53 Interesting Communication Exercises for Science Students

Sue Habeshaw
Senior Lecturer and Course Adviser
University of the West of England, Bristol

Di Steeds
Subeditor,
European Journal of Biochemistry

First published in 1987 by
Technical and Educational Services Ltd.
37 Ravenswood Road
Bristol BS6 6BW
U.K.

ISBN 0 947885 21 8

Printed in Great Britain by The Cromwell Press, Melksham, U.K.

Distributed by
Plymbridge Distributors Ltd., Estover Road, Plymouth PL6 7PZ
☎ (0752) 695745 *fax* (0272) 695699

INTERESTING WAYS TO TEACH

53 Interesting
Communication Exercises
for Science Students

January '95

Books from Technical & Educational Services

Preparing to teach: *An introduction to effective teaching in higher education*
53 Interesting things to do in your lectures
53 Interesting things to do in your seminars and tutorials
53 Interesting ways to assess your students
53 Interesting ways of helping your students to study
53 Interesting communication exercises for science students
53 Interesting ways to appraise your teaching
53 Interesting ways to promote equal opportunities in education
53 Interesting ways to teach mathematics
53 Interesting ways to write open learning materials
253 Ideas for your teaching
Interesting ways to teach: *7 Do-it-yourself training exercises*
Creating a teaching profile
Getting the most from your data: *Practical ideas on how to analyse qualitative data*
Writing study guides
Improving the quality of student learning
53 Problems with large classes: *Making the best of a bad job*

Acknowledgements

We would like to thank the following people for their help and
support in the production of this book
Cait Habeshaw
John Steeds.

We also thank the following for permission to include their
exercises in this collection
Jo Corke
Eira Makepeace
Teresa Wood

We are grateful to the following publishers for permission to
reprint their material
Hodder and Stoughton Ltd
The National Consumer Council
Pergamon Press Ltd
The Royal Society of Chemistry
Technicon Instruments Co. Ltd

Special thanks are due to Morgan and Grundy Ltd
for their help with exercise 38.

About the series

This book is the fifth in the series, *Interesting Ways to Teach*. These books are intended for teachers in further and higher education, though they are equally suitable for nurse tutors, management trainers and instructors on government training projects. Teachers in schools, too, will be able to adapt the material to their own situations.

The purpose of the series is to provide teachers with practical ideas for their teaching. While there are sound theoretical justifications for the suggestions (and occasionally even empirical evidence in their support) the emphasis throughout is on practice. The methods have all been tried out, and seen to work, by the authors.

The authors run workshops in the methods described in the books and full instructions for do-it-yourself training workshops are obtainable from the publishers.

Introduction

Teaching communication skills to science students can be a disheartening experience. Those teachers who are scientists themselves may feel they lack the necessary communication skills and teachers without a science background may find it difficult to relate the course to the needs of the students. With this in mind we have put together a collection of exercises which focus on those communication skills which science students most need and which are also largely based on science-related topics and scientific materials.

Some of the exercises are for use in the classroom while others are more suitable for setting as course work assignments and examination questions. They also vary in length: some can be dealt with quite quickly while others involve several hours of students' time.

This is a book for dipping into: each of the fifty-three items is written to make sense on its own. Each item includes a set of instructions for running the exercise and, where relevant, additional explanatory notes for non-scientists and materials for teachers to use or adapt. The materials are indicated by boxes drawn in the text.

If you want to photocopy the materials, copyright is waived in all cases except exercise 8. You will probably want to use an enlarging photocopier, particularly for handouts which students are expected to write on.

Because students studying in different areas have different needs you will sometimes want to devise your own materials for an exercise, using ours as a model. Suggestions for doing this are included where relevant. We hope that you and your students will find these exercises enjoyable as well as helpful.

Introduction to the second edition

Our original intention not to reprint this volume has been revised as a consequence of the continuing demand from teachers of science and communication studies. This decision was not taken lightly as we are aware that some of the exercises are dated. However, teachers have shown themselves to be quite capable of adapting the exercises to suit their own circumstances and we are confident that, where the materials need amendment, they will continue to do so.

Sue Habeshaw, Di Steeds July 1993

CONTENTS

Data presentation and interpretation

The arrangement of data in tables

Oral presentations

Self presentation

COMMUNICATION THEORY
(exercises 1 - 5)

A consideration of theory helps students to understand the principles of a subject and gives a basis and a coherence to the skills which are being taught.

A consideration of communication theory in particular helps students to take a fresh look at a subject which they have been practising, without thinking much about it, for the whole of their lives. It also has the incidental benefit that it gives this subject more status in their eyes: if it has theory it's not 'just common sense'.

The exercises in communication theory which are described here offer alternatives to the lecture as a way of teaching the material. They require the students to be involved, to participate and to think things out for themselves.

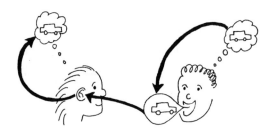

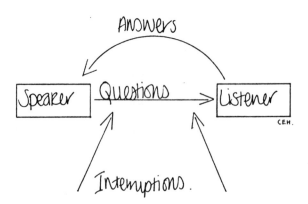

Communication models: two examples drawn by students

Communication models 1

Most communication courses involve a consideration of communication models. A range of models has been developed, many of which are based on the early model devised by Shannon and Weaver[1] to illustrate the process of communication by radio. More recent examples include Dance's helical model of communication[2], and Newcomb's triangular model[3].

Science students in particular often take to this kind of exercise because on their courses they are accustomed to dealing with interpretations of complex systems involving models.

If, rather than just showing these models to your students, you encourage them to find their own way of illustrating the communication process, they will not only benefit from participating and thinking things through for themselves, but also they will produce an interesting and varied set of ideas.

How to run the exercise

a   Ask your students to draw a communication model or, if that strikes them as being too difficult, suggest that they find some way of illustrating, diagrammatically or pictorially, the communication process. To make it easier for them you could recommend that they focus on what happens when two people have a conversation.

b   Tour the room, encouraging your students and looking out for examples which you can mention later if they are too reticent to talk about them themselves.

c   When they have all got something on paper, ask them in turn to show their illustration to the rest of the group. If the group is small and they are sitting in a circle, they can do this by holding up their papers in turn. If the group is too large for this to be possible, you can select individuals whose work illustrates a variety of approaches to draw their model on the board.

d   You can then show them the published models for comparison.

Getting the most out of the exercise

a   Encourage your students to consider how the theoretical models apply to their own experience. For instance you could ask them to think of examples of one-way and two-way communication. Or you could suggest that they adapt their diagrams to given situations, e.g. science lectures, television broadcasts etc.

b   This exercise will make more sense to students if it is not treated in isolation but followed up with other exercises on theory (e.g. exercises 2 and 3).

1   C. Shannon and W. Weaver, *The Mathematical Theory of Communication*, University of Illinois Press, Illinois, 1949

2   F.E.X. Dance, 'Toward a Theory of Human Communication' in F.E.X. Dance (ed.) *Human Communication Theory*, Holt, Rinehart & Winston, New York, 1967

3   T. Newcomb, *Psychological Review*, 60, 393-400, 1960

Communication barriers 2

The concept of communication barriers is one of the areas of theory which students relate to most easily. They usually have no difficulty in providing examples of things which get in the way of effective communication.

How to run the exercise

a Ask your students to suggest examples of barriers which could impede communication between two people. You could start them off by giving a couple of examples of your own, e.g. one person doesn't like the other, one person is deaf etc. Write all the examples on the board.

b Tell your students that together you are going to group the examples and ask them for ideas for grouping. Or, if you prefer, suggest headings yourself, such as 'linguistic barriers', 'psychological barriers', 'social barriers' etc. Group the examples under the headings, allowing plenty of time for discussion and disagreement.

c Set your students a short piece of writing entitled 'Communication barriers at college' (or 'Communication barriers at work' in the case of day-release or sandwich students). Suggest that they describe some of the barriers they have noticed and propose some ways of overcoming them. You will find that they will produce thoughtful and vivid work.

Getting the most out of the exercise

a This piece of writing, if it is set early in the course, can be useful diagnostically.

b You can make links between this exercise and others relating to theory by, for example, getting your students to add barriers to their communication models (see exercise 1) or by highlighting the potential of certain kinds of non-verbal communication as barriers (see exercise 5).

Defining communication 3

Defining terms is an essential part of any consideration of theory. And attempting to define communication can lead to an interesting and profitable discussion. This exercise uses test cases to explore these definitions.

How to run the exercise

a   Give your students a set of test situations such as:

you try to telephone someone and get the wrong number;

you try to telephone someone and don't get through;

you are speaking in your sleep and someone hears you;

you overhear two people speaking to each other;

someone throws a brick at you;

you are passing a building site and one of the workers accidentally dislodges a brick, which hits you;

someone says something to you and you don't hear;

someone says something to you and you misunderstand;

someone speaks to you in a language which you don't understand;

a television is on in an empty room.

b   For each situation ask your students, 'Is this an example of communication?' If they say yes ask them why; if they say no ask them why not. Encourage them to participate by explaining that these examples are problematic and capable of various interpretations.

c   As the discussion proceeds, you can take a summarising and challenging role. For example, if your students identify intention as a necessary condition for communication (as in the two examples involving bricks), you can highlight this and ask them to consider how the concept of intention applies in the telephoning and overhearing examples, for instance.

d   You can also encourage your students to contribute their own examples of test cases.

Getting the most out of the exercise

a   This exercise will have been successful if at the end of it your students have a sense of the complexity of the topic and the problems of agreeing on definitions in this area.

b   This exercise forms a good pair with exercise 1, which tends to have the opposite effect, as it simplifies the communication process.

Different types of communication   4

Many books on communication include charts or lists to show the range of different types of communication, sometimes with sections specifying advantages and disadvantages of each type.

You could, if you wished, give your students copies of such a chart. But they are, in fact, perfectly capable of drawing one up for themselves. And if they do it themselves, they will put more thought into it and learn more from it.

How to run the exercise

a   Give your students copies of the blank chart and get them to fill it in.

b   You can then either take in the charts and mark them or draw up a class chart on the board using your students' suggestions or ask your students to make joint charts in small groups on pieces of flip-chart paper.

Complete the chart: Use an extension sheet if necessary

Type of communication	Advantages	Disadvantages	Conditions for effective communication
Spoken			
Written			
Body language			
Other			

Body language 5

A study of non-verbal communication not only gives students a better understanding of their own and other people's body language but also, in the case of biology students in particular, offers opportunities to make links and comparisons between human and animal behaviour.

There is no need to lecture to students about non-verbal communication: you need only ask the right questions and they will draw on their own ample experience to find the answers. In fact, this exercise is a good one to use if you want to introduce students to the practice of working in groups independently of their teacher.

How to run the exercise

a   Before the session, make one copy of each of the work sheets.

b   List the headings on the board:

    Bodily contact

    Proximity etc.

Tell the students that these are headings which Michael Argyle originally used in his book *Social Interaction* [1] and explain each one very briefly, e.g. 'Bodily contact is to do with people touching each other. Proximity is to do with how close people get to each other' etc. If you are unsure of some of the meanings yourself, you can check them out in the book or in Michael Argyle's more recent book, *The Psychology of Interpersonal Behaviour* [2].

c   Distribute the copies of the work sheets around the class. Get students to work in pairs or threes with one or two sheets per group depending on the size of the class. Give them the following instructions: 'On these sheets you will find questions for you to answer and experiments for you to do. You don't need to restrict yourselves to what is on the sheet, though: feel free to discuss your group's topic in any way you want. Invent new experiments if you like. It's important, though, before you start, that you choose one member of your group to act as reporter and write down people's good ideas because in 20 minutes you will be asked to report back to the rest of the class'.

d After 20 minutes give the class the following instructions: 'Now each group is going to tell us about the discussion they've been having. We'll take the topics in the order in which I've listed them on the board. So we'll start with bodily contact...' The timing for this stage will need to be planned carefully. You will need to decide whether you want discussion after each report or after all the reports have been made and then divide the time accordingly, gently reminding people if they exceed their time allowance.

1 M. Argyle, *Social Interaction,* Methuen, London, 1969
2 M. Argyle, *The Psychology of Interpersonal Behaviour,* 4th edn, Penguin, Harmondsworth, 1983

Non-verbal communication : 1

Bodily contact

1 What are the rules governing bodily contact in our society?

2 Look round this room. Is anybody touching anybody else?

3 *Experiments*

    a Hold your neighbour's hand. Describe your feelings.

    b Touch someone from another pair. Observe his/her reaction. Ask him/her to describe his/her feelings.

4 Relate your discussion to what you know about animal behaviour.

Non-verbal communication : 2

Proximity

1 What determines how close a person will come to another in our society? Give examples.

2 *Experiment*

    Carry on a conversation with a partner, standing

    a too close for comfort;

    b too far apart for comfort.

    Describe your feelings.

3 What do you know about proximity behaviour in animals?

Non-verbal communication : 3

Orientation

1 Discuss the orientation of two people in an interview, in a restaurant and in a pub.

2 Comment on the orientation of people in this room.

3 Compare the orientation of students and teacher in a lecture and in a seminar. What effect does orientation have on communication?

4 *Experiment*

Turn your backs on the rest of the group and wait for comments.

Non-verbal communication : 4

Posture

1 What can posture communicate?

2 What can you infer from the posture of people in this room?

3 *Exercise*

Practise:

a tense and relaxed postures;

b welcoming and rejecting postures.

4 How do animals use posture to communicate?

Non-verbal communication : 5

Physical appearance

1   What can you infer from looking at the physical appearance (clothes, hairstyle etc.) of people in this room?

2   Think back to your first impressions when you met the others. Do you think that your first impressions were right?

3   *Exercise*
    Describe somebody you know. Which elements of the description are most important to you?

4   What can animals communicate with their physical appearance?

Non-verbal communication : 6

Facial expression

1   What roles does facial expression play in communication?

2   *Exercise*
    How many different emotions can you convey with your facial expression? Demonstrate them to your partner.

3   *Experiment*
    What can you infer about the people in this room from their facial expressions? Check to see if you are right by asking them.

Non-verbal communication : 7

Hand movements

1   Make a list of generally accepted messages which can be conveyed by the hands.

2   What can you infer from the ways in which people in this room are using their hands? (Look particularly for hand-to-head and hand-to-face movements.)

Head movements

3   What are the people in this room conveying with the positions and movements of their heads?

Non-verbal communication : 8

Direction of gaze

1   *Exercise*

Have a conversation with your partner and stare into his/her eyes all the time. Describe your feelings.

2   What are the rules governing the direction of gaze of two people in conversation? (Watch two people talking. Do they look more at each other when listening or speaking?)

3   What can animals communicate through gaze?

Non-verbal communication : 9

General

1 What non-verbal signs are there to indicate who is the teacher and who are the students in this room? (Use the list on the board for reference.)

2 What behaviour is expected in a teacher which is not acceptable in a student and vice versa?

THINKING ABOUT SCIENCE
(exercises 6 - 11)

There is so much information to acquire in a science subject that a student can follow a course for years without ever considering science in its social context or seeing it as an intellectual discipline with its own philosophy, rules and language. The exercises in this section are designed to start students thinking about science in this broader way.

Though these exercises are based in the philosophy of science, they are simple and accessible and require the students to reflect on the subject rather than learn any elaborate theory.

The exercises encourage students to see themselves as science students, to adopt a critical attitude to their subject and to consider how their studies relate to life outside the educational institutution. They also help them to find ways of communicating this.

Zen and the art of scientific   6
investigation

One of the clearest and most accessible introductions to scientific method can be found at the beginning of chapter 9 in *Zen and the Art of Motor Cycle Maintenance* by Robert M. Pirsig[1]. The author uses the example of locating a fault in a motor cycle to illustrate inductive and deductive logic and the process of scientific method. His style of writing is direct and attractive and the passage can be used in an introductory session on the nature of scientific investigation.

How to run the exercise

a Tell the group that they are going to investigate the *process* which they follow when they undertake a genuine scientific investigation.

b Explain that you do not want to complicate matters by using laboratory material which may be obscure to some of the group, (it is possible that your class is a mixed group of chemists, physicists etc.) so you are going to ask them to apply the scientific process to a non-scientific topic.

c Read out the passage from *Zen and the Art of Motor Cycle Maintenance,* the section which begins 'When you've hit a really tough one' on p.100 and ends almost halfway down p. 103. Point out that this offers an example of the sort of thing you mean.

d Ask everyone to write their own account of an investigation where observations are made, a hypothesis proposed, tests devised and a conclusion reached, stressing that the example should be from outside the laboratory. You might suggest some particularly bizarre problems just to encourage them to broaden their ideas here; for example, 'I am ill today because I went to the new restaurant last night', or 'I inherited my skill at juggling from my great-uncle'.

Getting the most out of the exercise

Like several of the exercises in this book (for example, exercises 38 and 49) this one approaches the problem of understanding a particular concept by asking students to apply that concept to unusual material. Once the material has been demystified the process for handling it can be seen more clearly.

You could also ask the class to point out when they use inductive and when deductive logic in their investigations. This exercise is a useful preparation for exercise 7.

1   R. M. Pirsig, *Zen and the Art of Motor Cycle Maintenance*, Corgi, London, 1981

Scientific method: 7
follow the chart

This is a useful follow-up exercise after the subject of scientific method has been introduced through exercise 6.

How to run the exercise

Hand round copies of the chart and allow up to 40 minutes for written answers to the questions.

Getting the most out of the exercise

It is worthwhile taking in and marking all the answers in this case, not only because some students may experience difficulty in recognising the difference between negative and inconclusive results (see exercise 33) but also because the answers to question 2 may well produce ma.erial which is worth discussing with the class.

Many science courses, for example, follow the chart exactly backwards. Students may well be first taught the theory and then told which experiments led to it and what were the hypotheses and predictions of the original experimenter. They will then be urged to 'look about them' and find examples of this effect - in other words to make some observations. It is hardly surprising, therefore, that when they attempt their own experiments and do not get the 'right' answer they are more likely to modify the observations than the hypothesis or the experiment.

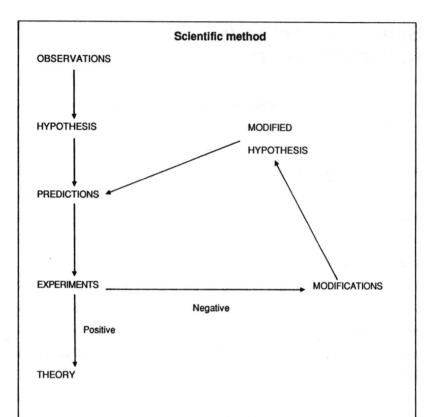

Scientific method

OBSERVATIONS

HYPOTHESIS   MODIFIED
                    HYPOTHESIS

PREDICTIONS

EXPERIMENTS ⟶ MODIFICATIONS

Negative

Positive

THEORY

1   The above diagram represents the process of scientific method. Give an account of a scientific investigation of your choice in terms of the headings of the diagram, showing how the investigation uses the process of scientific method.

2   How far does the way in which you work on this course or in your job follow scientific method?

Jumping to conclusions 8

The dangers and attractions of abandoning the process of scientific method are demonstrated in this exercise.

How to run the exercise

Ask the group to read the extract from *Supernature* by Lyall Watson[1], and answer the three questions. You could ask them to prepare individual written answers or suggest a discussion in small groups, which report back to the class after about 20 minutes.

Getting the most out of the exercise

a The first two questions make this as much a study of scientific language as an exercise in method. There is a potent mixture of technical terms, such as 'psychogalvanic-reflex electrodes' and 'Faraday screen', jargon abbreviations ('PGR') and a Latin name *('Dracaena massangeana')* with emotive language such as 'a discovery that changed his life' and 'torture'. (See section on the language of science.)

b The third question requires an understanding of the value of scientific method. There are unjustifiable assumptions made in stating the problem. The assumption that a plant can be *tortured* begs the question and presupposes the conclusion, which is that a plant can perceive the intent to harm. The hypothesis is, therefore, inappropriate and the experiment fails because it does not adequately test the hypothesis. However, there is the potential for a genuine experiment here, inspired by real observations, and students from all scientific disciplines should be able to devise interesting hypotheses which can be tested experimentally.

Devising your own materials

There is a good essay by James Oberg[2] about the tendency of investigators into the paranormal to reject scientific method which you might find a useful starting point for further exercises of this sort.

1 L. Watson, *Supernature*, Hodder and Stoughton, London, 1973
2 J. Oberg, *New Scientist*, 84, 102-105, 1979

The following experiment aroused considerable popular interest. Read the passage and then answer the questions.

On a February morning in 1966 Cleve Backster made a discovery that changed his life and could have far-reaching effects on ours. Backster was at that time an interrogation specialist who left the CIA to operate a New York school for training policemen in the techniques of using the polygraph, or "lie detector". This instrument normally measures the electrical resistance of the human skin, but on that morning he extended its possibilities. Immediately after watering an office plant, he wondered if it would be possible to measure the rate at which water rose in the plant from the root to the leaf by recording the increase in leaf-moisture content on a polygraph tape. Backster placed the two psychogalvanic-reflex (PGR) electrodes on either side of the leaf of *Dracaena massangeana*, a potted rubber plant, and balanced the leaf into the circuitry before watering the plant again. There was no marked reaction to this stimulus, so Backster decided to try what he calls "the threat-to-well-being principle, a well-established method of triggering emotionality in humans". In other words he decided to torture the plant. First of all he dipped one of its leaves into a cup of hot coffee, but there was no reaction, so he decided to get a match and burn the leaf properly. "At the instant of this decision, at 13 minutes and 55 seconds of chart time, there was a dramatic change in the PGR tracing pattern in the form of an abrupt and prolonged upward sweep of the recording pen. I had not moved, or touched the plant, so the timing of the PGR pen activity suggested to me that the tracing might have been triggered by the mere thought of the harm I intended to inflict on the plant.".... Enclosing the plant in a Faraday screen or a lead container has no effect, and it seems that the signals to which it responds do not fall within the normal electromagnetic spectrum. In more recent experiments Backster has found that fresh fruit and vegetables, ·mold cultures, amoebae, paramecia, yeast, blood, and even scrapings from the roof of a man's mouth all show similar sensitivity to other life in distress.

Lyall Watson, *Supernature,* Hodder and Stoughton, London, 1973

1 How does the language used in the passage help to convince a reader that the experiment is significant? Pick out the words and phrases which illustrate the points you make.

2 To what extent is the language scientific?

3 Suggest an alternative hypothesis to Backster's claim that the plant perceived his intention to inflict harm. How might you test your hypothesis?

Science and society 9

It is useful for science students to consider relationships between science and society and to be aware of how scientific theories are reflected in society. And it is important that they recognise that they have a responsibility to challenge popular misrepresentations of scientific thinking.

This exercise involves applying a scientific theory to aspects of human society and encourages students to look at these connections and misrepresentations. It also helps them to develop the skills of application which are crucial to scientific thinking.

How to run the exercise

a   Give the students copies of the exercise or, if you prefer, write it on the board.

b   Divide the students into working groups or pairs. Assign one of the categories (a - g) to each pair or group of students and give them 10 minutes to prepare a statement. Remind them that one person in the group should make notes on the discussion as they go along.

c   After 10 minutes ask for a report from each group.

d   Encourage discussion.

Getting the most out of the exercise

The discussion of this exercise can be very fruitful. Look out for signs of deterministic thinking: students using the word 'natural' to justify a weak argument, for example, or assuming that something is inevitable because it is backed up by scientific theory.

Encourage them to challenge the application of the theory to human society and to examine social and political implications of its misapplication.

Devising your own materials

Although a biological theory is used for this exercise you could equally well take as your example a theory from physics, chemistry etc. if your students are not studying biology. For example, 'everything tends towards disorder' or 'to every action there is an equal and opposite reaction'.

Look for ideas in the courses which your students are following. If you are not a scientist yourself, ask your colleagues for suggestions. Your students will probably have some good ideas, too, particularly if you ask them when they have done the exercise once and know what is involved.

Science and society

The hypothesis

Darwin's theory of natural selection can equally be applied to aspects of human society.

Testing the hypothesis

In groups, test the application of the hypothesis to

a   transport

b   racism

c   private enterprise

d   languages

e   political parties

f   education

g   sport.

Scientific debate 10

It is important that science students are given the opportunity to spend time in a structured situation exploring the implications of their commitment to science. Since this opportunity is not normally offered as part of the science curriculum, it generally falls to communication teachers to provide it.

The debate format may seem too formal for the modern classroom but science students, who are not used to being asked for their views and opinions, can find such a structure very helpful.

How to run the exercise

a   Select a topic for debate. This can be chosen by you or selected by the students. There may be a scientific controversy currently in the news which you can take advantage of. Some perennial topics for debate in science are:

vivisection

nuclear power

genetic engineering

science and neutrality

science and certainty

the funding of scientific research.

The topic is best phrased as a statement (as in traditional motions for debate) or as a question: 'Nuclear power is not worth the risk' or 'Do we want nuclear power?'

b   Divide the class into two groups. Ask one group to prepare arguments for the motion and the other to prepare arguments against. They will need 15-20 minutes for this. (You can divide a large class into four groups and debate two motions.)

c Bring the two groups together and start debating. You may want to set up a formal debate with a proposer and seconder for and against the motion, or you may prefer a less traditional structure with, for example, one student from each side in turn presenting an argument for discussion. Or you may find that, when students have had the opportunity to prepare their arguments beforehand, they engage quite happily in an unstructured discussion.

d It is probably helpful if you act as chairperson on the first occasion to demonstrate the role; when students are used to debating, one of them can take over the chair.

Getting the most out of the exercise
A good debate can form the basis for very interesting written work.

Definitions of science 11

Science students deal with definitions all the time but they may never have considered defining science itself. This exercise encourages them to think about science and to be aware of what their preoccupations are as science students and how these differ from those of students on other courses. It may also help them in a general way to make more sense of what they are doing on their course.

How to run the exercise

a   Ask your students each to write a short definition of science. (They should have no difficulty in understanding the task though they will need time to think of their reponses.)

b   Either ask them to read out their definitions in turn (if the group is small) or take in their definitions and reproduce a copy of the total set for each student.

c   Set up a discussion of the definitions. You could prompt if necessary with such questions as

'Which definition is the one which most members of the general public would agree with?'

'Do some of these definitions apply more to some branches of science than others?'

'What is the point of defining science?'

'Is science really as certain as these definitions suggest?'

'How do these definitions of science relate to science as it is taught on your course?'

STUDY SKILLS
(exercises 12 - 15)

As it is well recognised that we learn best when there is a perceived need to learn and that study skills classes will be the first ones that students avoid when they fall behind in their studies, we have limited ourselves to exercises which relate most closely to scientific coursework.

So I'll give you the time now 12

As often as one urges students to read through lecture notes immediately after a lecture and sort out the confusing points one hears the objection 'But there isn't time'. This brief exercise offers students the chance to review lecture notes and demonstrates that the process need only take a few minutes.

How to run the exercise

a Ask the students to take out the notes from their last (or another appropriate) lecture.

b Give them 5 minutes to read them through.

c Ask if anyone has discovered any omissions, inconsistencies or incomprehensible material, suggesting that they ask the person sitting next to them for help. This need only take 2 or 3 minutes.

d Now give time for any unanswered questions to be discussed by the class as a whole.

e If some points are still unclear help the students to formulate the questions which they need to ask and decide how they might best be answered. You could say 'Does anyone know which book would deal with this topic? Have you got a copy with you?' or 'Is this a question which you should ask your teacher? Will someone volunteer to ask her and report back to the class?'

Getting the most out of the exercise

a You might decide to run this exercise routinely using, say, the first 10-15 minutes of every communication session.

b   It is possible that a general discussion on notetaking and other relevant skills
could develop and start to take over all the time available. If this happens you
might consider postponing your original plans for the session; it could be a
rare opportunity to talk about study skills with a motivated group.

Essay writing   13

If you are not a scientist you may feel unable to offer constructive help with scientific essays.   Indeed, even if you are trained in one of the sciences you may still know very little about the specialist course which your students are following. In fact most of the essays which science students have to write will probably be straightforward accounts of factual material, with which they require little help, but this means that they have little or no practice in writing a genuinely discursive essay.   When they are set this type of essay, therefore, they may feel unprepared.

This exercise organises the students' own material into a plan for a 'compare and contrast' type of essay.

How to run the exercise

a   Ask the science staff to suggest some appropriate essay titles.

b   Have ready one or two titles of your own, which are so general that nobody will be able to claim that they simply don't know anything about any of them. You might try, for instance, 'Science is the only truth. Discuss' or 'Women need women doctors'.

c   Hand round copies of the list of titles or put them up on the board. You might like to ask the group how they feel about the task of choosing and writing one of these essays.

d   Check that everyone can recognise that titles of this sort require a discursive answer. In other words, make it clear that a title such as 'The value of.

cytogenetics in modern medicine' implies 'Assess the value of cytogenetics..'
and that 'Women need women doctors' is really asking 'How far do women
need women doctors?'

e   Take the students through the nine stages of 'A strategy for planning a
discussion essay'. It is better to present and deal with these one by one; you
can assure the class that they will be given copies outlining the whole
process at the end of the session.

f   Find out whether the members of the group now feel more confident about
tackling an essay of this sort.

Getting the most out of the exercise

a   Essay titles often use the word 'discuss' when they mean 'describe', as in
'Discuss the behaviour of proteins in solution'. You might point this out to
your students while taking care not to include a title of this sort in your list for
this exercise.

b   When dealing with stage 3 in the 'Strategy' it is a good idea to stress the
importance of the *facts*. Students encouraged to offer opinions may well
forget that these must be based on evidence.

c   Stages 4 and 6 may require some discussion. Any decision about the order
of the material (stage 4) will determine the appropriate 'flagging'. If, for
example, they decide to deal first with all the points on one side of the
argument and to follow these with all the opposing points (effectively dividing
the essay into two halves) it is important to signal this in the introduction to
prevent the reader from spending half the essay thinking that it is biased or
unperceptive. If, however, the points for and against alternate in the essay,

54

phrases such as 'on the other hand' must be used in each paragraph to prevent an impression of inconsistency.

d   A variation on this exercise would be to get the whole class to work together on planning the essay. Ask them to 'brainstorm' on the chosen topic while you note down all their ideas on the board. You could attempt to sort them as they are suggested but it is probably easier to do this as a separate process.

e   If you still feel uneasy about handling technical material what about asking one of their science staff to find you an excellent essay of this type written by a former student or a student in a different group? By becoming familiar with this essay beforehand you may feel more confident when your group makes its own attempt at the same title.

A strategy for planning a discussion essay

1 Note points for and against in two columns.

2 Rank the points for and against in order of importance: 1,2,3.

3 For each point make brief notes on the facts it will contain and your discussion of them.

4 Decide on an order for your material. Should you deal first with all the 'points for' (in order of importance) and follow this with all the 'points against' or should you alternate your points for and against?

5 Decide on the conclusion.

6 Consider the 'flagging' which will be needed to help a reader to follow your argument. Make it clear whether you are citing evidence, drawing a reasoned conclusion or putting a counter argument by using phrases such as:

> This clearly demonstrates that...
>
> It has been argued that...
>
> Evidence seems to point to...
>
> On the other hand...
>
> However, this conflicts with...
>
> There is a widely held view that...

7 Decide whether to use subheadings.

8 Write a draft introduction.

9 Check your plan with a friend and ask for comments.

Reading a scientific article   14

Students are frequently asked to read the current literature or prepare a seminar paper based on an article in a scientific journal long before they feel able to assess new work critically. They may not even know where current issues and back numbers of journals are kept in the library (see exercises 16 - 18) and the structure of a published research paper may be strange to them.

The discovery that such articles almost always contain abstracts or summaries may seem to relieve the problem but these are not adequate for a critical appreciation of the work.

One excellent way of penetrating a difficult paper is to ask oneself specific questions as one reads through, such as those devised by Deborah Mowshowitz and Barbara Filner[1], and these form the basis of the list of questions used in this exercise.

How to run the exercise

a   Obtain copies of one or several journal articles, recommended by the science department as relevant to students at this stage of their course.

b   You could ask the class how they feel about the prospect of reading the articles critically.

c   Now hand round copies of the exercise which follows and ask the class to answer the questions, suggesting that they do this   individually, asking questions of each other or the whole group when they get stuck. Material for evaluating the article may well be generated when members of the group question each other in this way.

d   When they have finished ask whether anyone now feels more able to cope with an article of this type.

Getting the most out of the exercise

Even if you are not a scientist, try and do the exercise yourself first; you'll be reassured to discover that the questions 'work'. You may well wish to modify the questions to make them more relevant to the chosen paper or to the stage students have reached in their course. For instance, question 5 might more usefully ask, 'What further information might you now look up to increase your understanding of this paper?' or 'What further experiments do you think would be worth doing to develop or test the ideas of this article?'

The time required for this exercise will depend on the length and complexity of the journal articles you use, but it can be quite demanding and take at least one hour. If you have to spread it over two separate sessions it is a good idea to begin by concentrating on question 2. Ask the group to skim-read the abstract and possibly the introduction, to put the work into context, and then ask them specifically to draw a flow diagram of the methods used. Flow charts are a very good way of summarising scientific procedure and some of the class may not have had much practice in constructing them. The remainder of the article can then be dealt with in the second session.

1   D. Mowshowitz and B. Filner, *Biochemical Education* , 7, 1979

Paper questions

The following questions are designed to help you read and analyse scientific papers. Sometimes the questions need to be asked only once for each paper, but often they need to be repeated for each experiment.

1 **Introduction** (why the authors did this set of experiments)

   a What are the authors trying to settle, prove or demolish? To put it another way, what question(s) are they asking?

   b How did this issue come up?

   c Why is it worth the effort to settle this issue?

   Note. It is sometimes easier to figure out why they did the experiments (1) *after* you figure out what they did (2). So if in doubt about 'why', attack 'what' first.

2 **Materials and methods** (what the authors actually did)

   a What did the authors measure?

   b What apparatus did they use (where relevant)?

3 **Results** (what happened)

   What were their results? (Summarise briefly.)

4 **Conclusions** (what can be concluded from the results)

   a What did these measurements enable the authors to calculate or estimate?

b What significance do they put on these results? How do they interpret their results?

5 Discussion (general)

What recommendations do they make for future work in this field?

Adapted from Deborah Mowshowitz and Barbara Filner,

Biochemical Education, 7, 1979

Understanding equipment 15

Students in laboratory classes are often required to use new pieces of equipment without being given adequate time to familiarise themselves with them first. When this happens, they feel confused and resentful and waste time asking laboratory staff for help.

One way they can familiarise themselves beforehand is by working with the manufacturer's manual.

This is an exercise which serves the dual purpose of giving students practice in writing summaries and familiarising them with the principles of a piece of equipment. The example used here is the AutoAnalyzer which is a standard piece of automated biochemical equipment. The material is drawn from the manufacturer's manual[1].

How to run the exercise

a Get your students to answer the question at the end of the passage. (Put a limit on the number of words they can use if you want.)

b The answers can be discussed in class or handed in for marking.

c This can lead to a discussion of the original material: for example, students can give a critique of the way in which it is written and make suggestions for improvement.

Devising your own materials

Unless your students happen to work with the AutoAnalyzer, you will probably need to use your own material to do this exercise. If you teach science yourself, you will know which piece of equipment to select. If you don't, your colleagues should be glad to help you with advice and materials, particularly since their practical classes will run more smoothly when students understand the principles of the equipment they are using. And you may like to borrow a white coat and go to the class with your students: you can learn a lot from attending a practical and observing what goes on.

1 *A Short Primer on the AutoAnalyzer,* Technicon Instruments Co. Ltd, Basingstoke, 1967

The AutoAnalyzer

Read these notes from *A Short Primer on the AutoAnalyzer* and answer the question at the end.

The AutoAnalyzer is a train of interconnected modules that automates the step-by-step procedures of clinical and industrial wet-chemical analyses. In AutoAnalysis, chemical reactions take place in continuously flowing, air-segmented streams. The flow of the stream (or streams) proceeds from module to module, each of which automatically carries out a different analytical function, such as sampling of unknowns and standards; metering of reagents; purification and filtration; heating and incubation; detection and recording.

Briefly, operation is as follows: After the samples are loaded into the cups on the sampler, a multiple-channel proportioning pump, operating continuously, moves the samples, one following another, and a number of streams of reagents, into the system. Sample and reagents are brought together under controlled conditions, causing a chemical reaction and color development. Color intensity of the analytical stream is measured in a colorimeter, the results appearing as a series of peaks on a recorder chart.

Air bubbles continously segment the flowing streams of samples and reagents, thereby maintaining sample integrity and eliminating cross-mixing of samples.

Fundamental to AutoAnalyzer techniques is the exposure of known standards to exactly the same reaction steps as the unknown samples. The concentration of the unknowns is continuously plotted against the known concentrations. For this reason (and herein lies the key to the rapid results attainable with the AutoAnalyzer), reactions need not be carried to completion as in conventional chemistry procedures. Detection devices include colorimetry, spectrophotometry, flame photometry, and atomic absorption spectrometry.

In this type of analysis, changeover from one clinical determination to another is only a matter of changing the chemical reaction occurring in the flowing stream (and this can be done in a matter of minutes).

In short, with a single AutoAnalyzer, it is possible for the clinical chemist or industrial analyst to automate a majority of the determinations he is called upon to perform.

A Short Primer on the AutoAnalyzer,
Technicon Instruments Co. Ltd, 1967

Q   What are the advantages of the AutoAnalyzer?

USING A LIBRARY
(exercises 16 - 18)

Introductory courses in library use are usually offered by the library staff during the first days of a student's course but you can follow those with projects which require students to use a wide range of the library facilities to obtain information which is particularly relevant to their work.

Exercises will, of course, vary with the type of library equipment available and the type of course being followed by the students. Full-time students may well use the college library exclusively and frequently whereas those following day-release courses may need to discover more generally what libraries can offer so that they can make the most of facilities at work or in their home town. However, the aim of the exercises is the same: to help your students to risk using new facilities in a strange library where everyone around is silent and looks competent.

I only wanted to borrow an audio cassette but there were so many interesting things — I stayed for a week!

Not only books I 16

This exercise was devised by Eira Makepeace, Bristol Polytechnic. It can be used by all students as a general introduction to library equipment and to approved ways of writing references.

How to run the exercise

a   Give your students copies of the instructions and, before dispatching them around the library, suggest that they do not all try to find the same items at the same time; this way the time available for using the equipment can be shared fairly.

b   Allow up to 1 hour for the library search and 20 minutes for a discussion afterwards.

Getting the most out of the exercise

a   Arrange to run this session at a time when the library staff are available to help.

b   Check in advance that the relevant equipment (microfiche readers, cassette players etc.) is in good working order.

c   You could ask your students to 'mark' each other's reference lists, checking for *consistency* of style.

Not only books I

1 Use the library catalogues and other sources of reference to identify the following:

    a   2 books which relate to your job/subject/interests;

    b   2 journal articles which relate to your job/subject/interests;

    c   2 items which relate to your job/subject/interests, which are not in a traditional format (for example, they might be on microfiche, microfilm, video or audio cassette).

2 Write full references to each of the above using the style of one of your chosen journals as your model.

Library and communication staff will be on hand to help you.

Not only books II   17

Although you will need to adjust this exercise to suit your particular library we hope that we have suggested the types of question which your students will find useful. This execise is based on questions devised by Teresa Wood, Bristol Polytechnic.

How to run the exercise

a   Give your students copies of the instructions and, before dispatching them round the library, suggest that they do not all try to find the same items at the same time; this way the time available for using the equipment can be shared fairly.

b   Allow up to 90 minutes for the library search and 20 minutes for a discussion afterwards.

Getting the most out of the exercise

a   Arrange to run this session at a time when the library staff are available to help.

b   Check beforehand that the relevant books and journals are on the shelves and that the equipment (microfiche readers etc.) is in good working order.

c   Since the students' reading lists are used in devising this exercise it is a useful way of discovering just how accessible are the books and journals which they need. The discussion may well reveal a need for the library to stock more copies of a key textbook or for the science staff to request that the most popular books be available only on short loan.

Not only books. II

Today's libraries offer more than books. How many of our library's facilities have you discovered? The aim of this exercise is to show you what we have and how to use it.

1 Using the visual display unit find this book.......................................

and answer the following questions:

   a   How many copies does the library possess?

   b   How many are issued?

   c   When are the copies due back?

   d   When is it possible to recall them?

2 The VDU only catalogues books which can be taken out of the library. Use the card index to discover whether there is a reference copy of the above book available.

3 Use *British Books in Print* (on microfiche) to choose a book you would like as a Christmas present. Find out (a) whether it is still in print; (b) the author; (c) the publisher; (d) the price.

4 The issue of *New Scientist* referred to in .... reading list (reference..) is held on microfilm. Find the article and answer the following questions.

5 Choose one of the videotapes recommended by .... Listen to it, making notes. Did you find any problems with your note taking? How might these be avoided?

6 Find the section of the library where the current copies of periodicals are displayed. What is the subject of the editorial in..............................?

     Library and communication staff will be on hand to help you.

Paper-chase

This exercise is based on guidelines devised by Jo Corke, Bristol Polytechnic, to introduce first year biology students to scientific journals.

How to run the exercise

a Choose a time when the library staff are available to help you.

b Give your students copies of the instructions and, before dispatching them round the library, you could suggest that they do not all try to find the same items at the same time; this way the time available for using the equipment can be shared fairly.

c Allow 60 to 90 minutes for the library search and 30 minutes for a discussion afterwards.

Devising your own materials

You will need to involve the science staff in devising questions which relate to their particular courses and in choosing the most appropriate journals, but you may well find that some of them welcome this session not only as a communication exercise but as a means of teaching a particular topic.

The exercise could be given a single theme, such as different practical techniques, and thus become part of a structured approach to independent learning.

Paper-chase

1   Find *The Journal of Applied Bacteriology.* What publications are on the shelf either side of this journal? What does this tell you about the system of placing journals in the library?

2   Would you expect to find *The Biochemical Journal* before or after *The Journal of Applied Bacteriology* ? Find this journal; does this confirm or alter your ideas about journal organisation in the library?

3   Choose one issue (or bound volume) of *The Journal of Applied Bacteriology* and find the list of contents. The titles of the articles are designed to be sufficiently detailed to give you an immediate idea of the subject matter. Look for key words such as

   a   the names of specific organisms, e.g. 'The incidence of *Salmonella* in animal feeds';
   b   the names of specific products, e.g. 'The long-term effect of kerosine pollution on the microflora of moorland soils';
   c   the names of specific microbial activities, e.g. 'The development of the anaerobic spoilage flora of meat stored at chill temperatures'.

From the issue you have selected, find three articles with titles demonstrating key words of types a - c above and write a reference to each of these using the journal's own format.

4 Answer the following questions about the organism named in one of your chosen references. (Use the summary of the article, the introduction or your microbiology textbook to help you.)

   a Is the organism under investigation an alga, fungus, bacterium or virus? Is your answer expected in view of the title of the journal?
   b If it is a bacterium find out a few taxonomic details, e.g. gram reaction, sporing ability, shape, habitat.
   c What particular aspect of this microbe's existence is being investigated?

5 Look up the reference list at the end of any paper in *The Biochemical Journal* and find a reference to a book. Cite a reference to a chapter of your microbiology text book to the format used by *The Biochemical Journal.*

6 Write down the abbreviated titles of *The Journal of Applied Biology* and *The Journal of Biochemistry*, as used by the two journals. Compare their reference lists. Do they use the same abbreviations for all journal titles?

THE LANGUAGE OF SCIENCE
(exercises 19 - 24)

Scientific language aims to be precise and objective. It uses units which are internationally understood to apply to defined physical circumstances and it uses the third person passive voice to convey the idea that procedures are entirely independent of the experimenter. This convention has important implications which can be illustrated by comparing the following pairs of statements.

1   The solution was shaken for 4 minutes.
     I shook the solution for 4 minutes.

2   A slight colour change was observed.
     I saw the colour change slightly.

3   There is a linear relationship between the points.
     I drew a straight line through the points.

4   Three rats were sacrificed.
     I killed three rats.

Scientists are, of course, well aware that statements such as 2 and 3 are not actually objective as they stand and have developed calibrated instruments and statistical tests to quantify their observations. Non-scientists, however, may not even be aware that such tests are available and have, therefore, to trust the conclusions of a scientist without being able to assess the evidence. This is a situation which is clearly open to abuse. A layperson knows that good scientists aim to be accurate and will tend to believe what they say. In addition he or she will probably not understand the technical vocabulary but may be impressed by such terms as X-ray spectroscopy, fast-atom bombardment, 3 million volts, particle accelerator; catastrophe theory. It is all too easy to be 'blinded by science'.

Having several times had the uncomfortable experience of hearing science students claim that jargon is great because it really impresses people, we have devised some exercises which aim to point out the use and abuse of scientific language.

Objectivity 19

The concept of objectivity is a crucial one for science students to grasp, if only because on it depend so many of the conventions of scientific writing. If students understand why they are being asked to avoid all direct mention of themselves and their views in their writing they will be more likely to produce acceptable work.

This exercise is in two parts: in the first part, the students are asked to think about the mechanisms of writing objectively; in the second part, they are asked to challenge the concept itself.

How to run the exercise
This exercise can either be set as a piece of written work (in class or in an exam) or it can form the basis for a class discussion. You may find it helpful to give your students copies of a journal article from which to draw their examples.

Q What methods do scientists use in order to be objective in their writing? How far is it possible to be completely objective?

Writing for an audience 20

Science students need all the practice they can get in familiarising themselves with scientific language, understanding its conventions and studying its applications.

One way of giving them this practice is to get them to compare two or three different pieces of scientific writing around a given theme. The passages for comparison can be drawn from different historical periods, as in exercise 19, or from different types of printed source, as in exercise 20.

How to run the exercise

a   Give your students copies of the first passage (from Darwin's *The Origin of Species*). Ask them to underline anything which strikes them as being 'unscientific'. When they have done this ask them to say what they have underlined and why. This can lead into a discussion about the need to write differently for different audiences and the problem of popularising scientific ideas without distorting them.

b   Hand out copies of the second piece ('Gene transfer to cereal cells mediated by protoplast transformation') and ask your students whether they understand it. If any of them do, you can ask them to explain it to the rest of the class; this will provide you with an example of 'conversational' scientific language. The discussion can then focus on the question of the necessity for pieces of writing which are so obscure as to be understood by only a minority of even the scientifically trained population.

Devising your own materials

An exercise of this kind will benefit your students most if the passages relate to the course they are following. So look out for relevant passages in books and journals.

It is interesting to contemplate a tangled bank, clothed with many plants of many kinds, with birds singing on the bushes, with various insects flitting about, and with worms crawling through the damp earth, and to reflect that these elaborately constructed forms, so different from each other, and dependent upon each other in so complex a manner, have all been produced by laws acting around us. These laws, taken in the largest sense, being Growth with Reproduction; Inheritance which is almost implied by reproduction; Variability from the indirect and direct action of the conditions of life, and from use and disuse; a Ratio of Increase so high as to lead to a Struggle for Life, and as a consequence to Natural Selection, entailing Divergence of Character and the Extinction of less-improved forms. Thus, from the war of nature, from famine and death, the most exalted object which we are capable of conceiving, namely, the production of the higher animals, directly follows. There is grandeur in this view of life, with its several powers, having been originally breathed by the Creator into a few forms or into one; and that, whilst this planet has gone cycling on according to the fixed law of gravity, from so simple a beginning endless forms most beautiful and most wonderful have been, and are being evolved.

Charles Darwin, *The Origin of Species*, John Murray, London, 1859

Summary. Direct gene transfer to cereal cells was achieved by transformation of protoplasts with naked DNA. Protoplasts isolated from cultured cells of *Triticum monococcum* were incubated in the presence of polyethylene glycol (PEG) with circular and linear plasmid DNA. The pBR322-derived plasmid, pBL1103-4, contained a selectable chimeric gene comprising the protein coding region of the Tn*5* aminoglycoside phosphotransferase type II gene (NPTII), the nopaline synthase promoter (pNOS) and the polyadenylation signal of the octopine synthase gene. Transformed cells were selected in medium containing kanamycin and identified by detection of aminoglycoside phosphotransferase II activity.

Horst Lörz, Barbara Baker and Jeff Schell, *Molecular and General Genetics,* 199, 178-182, 1985

The popularisation of science 21

Science is often in the news. Many scientific developments and controversies are considered of sufficient general interest to be covered not only by specialist journals but also by the daily press.

It can be instructive for students to make a comparison between the specialist and the popular versions: as well as highlighting the characteristics of scientific writing, this can raise issues around the popularisation of science.

How to run the exercise

a Look out for reports on scientific topics in the daily papers. Keep the newspaper pieces and then track down the original journal articles. (*The Times* science correspondent always gives the reference.)

b Show your students copies of two accounts: a newspaper report and a journal article.

c Ask them questions which encourage them to engage with the materials and consider the issues raised. These questions will clearly vary depending on your choice of materials but they could include such examples as:

Why are these pieces written in such different ways?

How could you improve on them?

Is the newspaper account a responsible version of the journal report?

The Bermuda Triangle 22

Old legends never die but they may acquire a convincing veneer of scientific language. We are grateful to Graham Massey who assembled the evidence to refute Charles Berlitz's claims for the Bermuda Triangle, which we use in this exercise.

How to run the exercise

a Prepare for this exercise by reading the article by Graham Massey entitled 'The Meretricious Triangle' (*New Scientist*, 75, 74-76, 1977) and, if possible, take a copy with you into this session.

b Obtain a copy of *Without a Trace* by Charles Berlitz (Granada, London, 1978).

c Locate the passages discussed at length in Graham Massey's article and select one to read to the group.

d Tell the group that the topic for this session will be the popularisation of science and that you want them to listen to a section from one of the books on the subject of unsolved scientific mysteries.

e Read the appropriate section to the class or ask the group to read the passage for themselves.

f Ask for people's reaction to what they have read or heard.

g Now read out Massey's refutation of Berlitz's claims.

h Now ask the group to identify aspects of the presentation in the book which make the account particularly convincing to a non-scientist. They could do this in twos or fours and report back to the group.

Making the most of the exercise

If several of the group are impressed by the first reading from the book this demonstrates most convincingly the power of manipulative language and the implication that a proper scientific investigation has taken place, when 'evidence' has been only selectively presented. It is, however, important that those who believed the account are not made to feel foolish. You could say, for example, 'I admit that I have pulled something of a confidence trick on you. This was because, although you are all scientists, I wanted to put you in the position of the general public, who believe scientists to be honourable - generally incomprehensible, but honourable'.

Exciting or exploiting? 23

One of the most successful exploiters of scientific language is the popular author Erich von Daniken. So outrageous are the claims made in his best-selling book *Chariots of the Gods?* that the BBC devoted a programme in the *Horizon* series to refuting them.

How to run the exercise

a Choose a passage from *Chariots of the Gods?* by Erich von Daniken (Corgi, London, 1971) to read to the class.

b Tell your students that you want them to identify the words and phrases which persuade the reader that the evidence is significant.

c They can start doing this directly or you can read out the passage quite rapidly to convey the overall direction of von Daniken's argument and then repeat the reading more slowly, asking the students to stop you whenever they want to comment on the language used. They might, for example, distinguish between the scientific and non-scientific wording in a sentence such as, 'the strength used was *0.000,000,000,000,000,01 watts,* an *almost incredibly* weak output' (our italics). (To nitpick: when a fraction of a unit, 10^{-17} Watt, is cited the unit must be singular; one says three-quarters of a mile not three-quarters of miles.)

d You might then extend the discussion to the author's tendency to make statements and draw dramatic conclusions without discussing the evidence; is this popularisation or misrepresentation? If such literary techniques have no place in scientific reports is scientific writing inevitably dull?

Science on television   24

People with scientific training often find themselves in the position of having to explain things in a simplified form to non-specialists. They can learn a lot during their training from taking a critical look at how this is done in science programmes on television which are produced for a mixed audience.

How to run the exercise

a   Choose a videotape of a television science programme such as *Horizon*. (The BBC will provide you with a list of videotapes available for purchase or hire.) Look for a topic which your students should know something about. View the video yourself before the class and make notes.

b   Tell your students the topic and ask them 'What problems do the makers of a *Horizon* programme have?' They will probably suggest such problems as the difficulty of a mixed audience of experts and non-experts, the tension between education and entertainment etc. List the problems on the board.

c   Then ask them 'What methods do the makers of a *Horizon* programme have for solving these problems?' Take each problem in turn and write the students' suggestions next to it.

d   Give the students a list of questions to ask themselves while they are watching the videotape. Ideally these will be based on the suggestions which they have made themselves but if you are short of time you can use a ready-made list. (A list of suggestions follows.)

e   Discuss the programme and the answers to the questions.

Getting the most out of the exercise

a   When your students criticise aspects of the programme, encourage them to suggest improvements and alternatives of their own.

b   You can follow this up by asking them to give their own short presentations of a scientific topic for a mixed audience. (And if you have the facilities you can record them.)

Questions to ask yourself

when watching the *Horizon* programme

How is the link person used?

How are the experts used?

How are complex ideas explained?

How is the scientific terminology introduced?

Are the analogies appropriate?

How is variety achieved?

How far is the visual potential of the medium exploited?

Are compromises made in the name of simplicity or entertainment?

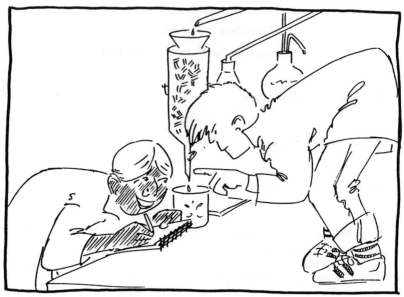

I think that's a hydrogen bond. Better put in a hyphen.

TECHNICAL WRITING
(exercises 25 - 29)

Technical language, units and formulae make special demands on written English, which test some of the conventional rules. So this section looks at the grammar and syntax of scientific writing.

Since all rules are most readily learned when one can see the reason for them we have used the notes which accompany exercise 24 to explain the logic behind some of the conventions.

Although we may be accused of nit-picking, we have found that these exercises run very successfully and produce constructive discussions.

What's the difference between ...?   **25**

Teachers of communication often receive requests from science staff to help students to write 'good English'. Exercises taken from English language text books, however, are not usually suitable for this purpose because they are too general and too juvenile. Exercises which acknowledge students' maturity and use scientific material are more likely to be acceptable to them.

This exercise gives students practice in dealing with scientific vocabulary. It consists of a set of pairs or groups of words, often used in scientific writing, which are easily confused by students because of a similarity in form or meaning.

How to run the exercise

a   Give your students a copy of the list.

b   Ask them, working individually or in pairs, to fill in the spaces on the list.

c   Discuss their answers with them.

d   You could then ask them to show that they know how to use the words in context by writing sentences illustrating their use.

Getting the most out of the exercise

This exercise will have more impact if it is followed up in your students' other written work. You can do this by drawing errors to students' notice and asking your colleagues to do the same.

What's the difference between ...?

In the spaces provided write the meanings of the words in such a way as to indicate the difference between them.

a   scarce ....

     rare ....

     unique ....

b   refute ....

     deny ....

     disprove...

c   accurate ....

     precise ....

     reliable ....

     exact ....

     specific ....

d   valid ....

     true ....

e   continuous ....

     continual ....

f opposite ....

   contrary ....

   contradictory ....

g alternative ....

   alternate ....

h significant ....

   important ....

i interpolate ....

   extrapolate ....

   deduce ....

j limited ....

   small ....

   minimal ....

k rudimentary ....

   vestigial ....

l .nfer ....

   imply ....

What's the plural of...?

This is the second of two exercises which give students practice in using scientific vocabulary. It consists of a list of words whose singular and plural forms can easily be confused because they are based on Latin or Greek.

How to run the exercise

a   Give your students a copy of the list.

b   Ask them to fill in the spaces. They can work on this individually or in pairs.

c   Ask them to give the answers or provide them yourself.

Getting the most out of the exercise

If you are to convince students that it is important to use the correct singular and plural forms of scientific terms, you and your colleagues will need to follow up this exercise by pointing out such errors when they occur in students' written work.

Devising your own materials

It may be that this particular list is not appropriate for your students. If this is the case, you can make your own list, preferably in consultation with the other members of staff who teach them. If you are not a science teacher you will probably find your colleagues' help particularly useful. You can also ask students to provide examples of their own.

What's the plural of...?

formula...

bacillus..

nucleus...

appendix...

focus..

locus..

hyperbola...

parabola...

index..

matrix..

maximum...

bronchus..

spectrum..

virus...

genus...

analysis...

axis..

helix..

What's the singular of...?

media...

bacteria.. ....

phenomena..

data...

criteria...

vertebrae...

antennae..

larvae...

A complex problem for copper! 27

In this exercise students learn the rules which govern the presentation of numerical quantities, technical terms, formulae and units in scientific writing. It is a bogus practical account of a real chemistry experiment (A-level standard).

How to run the exercise

a Explain to the class that you are going to give them copies of a supposed practical account, which has been very badly written.

b Hand round copies of the exercise which follows, the version without the superscripts which mark the deliberate mistakes.

c Tell everyone that the results are factually correct, as is the conclusion that the observations indicate the formation of a complex, and that their job is to identify all the errors of literary and scientific style.

d You can now simply go around the class in turn, asking each student to point out a mistake, explain what is wrong and correct it.

e There is not much to be gained by asking the class to rewrite the whole report. They would almost certainly eliminate most of the errors by totally rephrasing the passage and it is much more valuable if each mistake is tackled individually.

Getting the most out of the exercise

The conventions of scientific writing are precise and logical but if you are a non-scientist you may not know why certain rules apply. The following notes identify all the mistakes and attempt to explain the thinking behind the rules while indicating the areas which are open to discussion.

A complex problem for copper![1]

Everyone knows[2] that copper hydroxide dissolves in acids, but few people understand its behaviour in an aqueous alkali situation.[3] We have discovered that it *can*[4] dissolve by means of employing the following methodology.[5]

Methods

9 ml.[6] of[7] 8 M pot.[8] hydroxide was taken from a polythene[9] bottle and added to 1 cm^3 [10] of a[11] 0.20 molar[12] $CuSO_4.5H_2O$ solution in a centrifuge tube. The solution was warmed to 30°[13], shaken and centrifuged for about 75.5 secs.[14] The spectrum was then measured on a Perkin-Elmer 402 Spectophotometer,[15] using the visible light range between 450-800[16] nms[17], and a one cm[18] path length[19] cell. As the fig.[20] shows there is an absorption maximum at 640. [21]

Results

When the admixture[22] of the two solutions was completed a beautiful[23] deep blue coloration[24] developed, indicating the formation of a complex. The PE-402[25] gave the following spectrum.

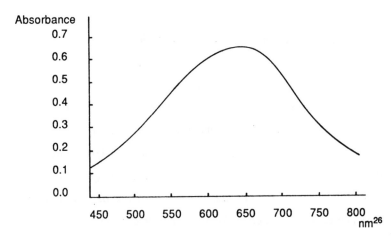

Fig. 1[27]

Discussion

It has been corroborated by other research groups that[28] anions of the form $Cu(OH)_3^-$ and $Cu(OH)_4^{2-}$ can exist in solution, and it is possible that one of these is responsible for the deep blue complex.

It is also possible that polymerization occurs, since hydroxide ions can easily form bridges, but at this moment in time[29] we are unable to make a clear statement on the precise nature of the formula of the complex. [30] We did, however, calculate its molar absorption coefficient (MAC) [31] since a 0.02 M copper solution had an absorption max.[32] of 0.64:

0.02 M complex gave 0.64 absorbance in 1 cm path

1 M complex gives 0.64/0.02 absorbance in 1 cm path

$$MAC = 32 \ M^{-1} \ cm^{-1} \ [33]$$

Notes

1   Uninformative jokey title with inappropriate exclamation mark.

2   Untrue.

3   This is obvious jargon; change to 'in aqueous alkali'.

4   Many quantities and symbols have to be in italics when scientific reports are printed; for instance [*methyl*-14C]methionine tells the reader that there is a 14C label in the existing methyl group of the methionine molecule; unitalicised the name would imply that an extra methyl group had been added to the molecule. For this reason italics (indicated by underlining in a hand-written copy) should be avoided as a means of merely emphasising a point.

5   An obviously clumsy phrase ending with 'methodology' misused; just say 'method'.

6   Abbreviations for units (e.g. ml cm m h) never have a full stop because the full stop, either on the line or above the line, is often used as a multiplication symbol.

7   There is a convention that if numerals and abbreviated units are used to express an amount of substance the words 'of' or 'of a' are omitted. The sentence should therefore begin '9 ml 8 M potassium hydroxide'.

8   As chemicals have their proper formulae (in this case KOH) there is no excuse for inventing one's own abbreviations. In fact the words 'potassium hydroxide' only occur once in this piece of writing so there is really no need for any abbreviation here at all.

9   Some of the students in your group may claim that we do not need to know what the bottle is made of. In fact 8 M potassium hydroxide will etch glass so

this is a useful piece of information if writing for a student or a non-specialist reader.

10 1 cm^3 is numerically equivalent to 1 ml and both cm^3 and ml have been used in the same sentence. You can choose to use either one, but it is important to be consistent.

11 See 7.

12 Molar is correctly abbreviated to M in the first line of Methods so for consistency it should be abbreviated here also.

13 30° C.

14 The abbreviation for second or seconds is s. Also, is it appropriate to say '*about* 75.5 s'?

15 There is no reason why spectrophotometer should start with a capital. The class may argue the pros and cons of including the maker's name for this instrument. In research papers this may give useful information about reliability, reproducibility or accuracy of results.

16 Either 'the visible light range of 450-800 nm' or 'the visible light range between 450 nm and 800 nm'.

17 Abbreviated symbols for units do not have an s at the end to make them plural. One writes 1 nm (nanometer) and 10 nm not 10 nms, since s can be confused with the abbreviation for seconds.

18 Either '1 cm' or 'one centimeter' but as the abbreviation cm has already been used this should be repeated for consistency.

19 The whole phrase describes the cell, therefore it ought to be hyphenated: '1-cm-path-length', which looks clumsy. What about changing it to 'a cell of 1 cm path length'?

20 Why abbreviate the word 'figure'?

21 640 nm (units must be given); shouldn't this statement be in Results?

22 'mixture' would be simpler and preferable.

23 Should the word 'beautiful' be used? This is worth discussing. In the simplest analysis it has no place in an objective scientific account; however, there are striking precedents for including terms which reveal the experimenter's attitude to his or her results. For example in the paper by Murray Gell-Mann, where he first predicts the existence of quarks (*Physics Letters*, 8, 214-215, 1964) he writes 'It is fun to speculate about the way quarks would behave...'.

24 Why not say 'colour'?

25 'spectrophotometer' would be better than coining the abbreviation 'PE-402'.

26 Axes of a graph should be labelled with a statement of what is being measured as well as the units of measurement, i.e. Wavelength (nm) or Wavelength/nm. (The absorbance on the vertical axis is correctly shown without units as it is dimensionless.)

27 A graph must have a descriptive title; in this case it could be 'Fig. 1. The absorbance spectrum of the suspected copper complex'.

28 Efforts to turn a practical account into the third person passive often lead students into clumsy constructions of this sort. Urge simplicity, such as the equally correct 'Other research groups have found that...'.

29 Jargon.

30 Jargon.

31 Is there any need for an abbreviation? In fact this quantity has an official abbreviation, ε (epsilon) so the term MAC should not be used, even though it

is defined.

32 Is there any need for an abbreviation?

33 There is an error in the argument which leads to the simple calculation. Although the original copper sulphate solution was diluted 1:10 and therefore became 0.02 M we can not know the molarity of the complex solution since we have no evidence for the formula of the complex. The calculation of a molar absorption coefficient is, therefore, spurious. This type of mistake is very common when someone, anxious to make the most of their results, loses sight of the limitations of the data. It is particularly easy to do this when the students 'know ' what the results of the experiment 'ought' to be. This is worth talking about.

A complex problem for copper!

Everyone knows that copper hydroxide dissolves in acids, but few people understand its behaviour in an aqueous alkali situation. We have discovered that it *can* dissolve by means of employing the following methodology.

Methods

9 ml. of 8 M pot. hydroxide was taken from a polythene bottle and added to 1 cm^3 of a 0.20 molar $CuSO_4.5H_2O$ solution in a centrifuge tube. The solution was warmed to 30°, shaken and centrifuged for about 75.5 secs. The spectrum was then measured on a Perkin-Elmer 402 Spectrophotometer, using the visible light range between 450-800 nms, and a one cm path length cell. As the fig. shows there is an absorption maximum at 640.

Results

When the admixture of the two solutions was completed a beautiful deep blue coloration developed, indicating the formation of a complex.

The PE-402 gave the following spectrum

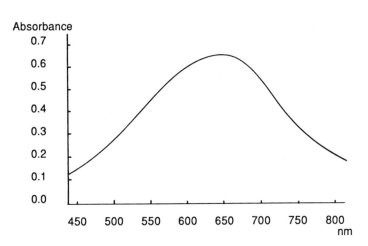

Discussion

It has been corroborated by other research groups that anions of the form $Cu(OH)_3^-$ and $Cu(OH)_4^{2-}$ can exist in solution, and it is possible that one of these is responsible for the deep blue complex. It is also possible that polymerization occurs, since hydroxide ions can easily form bridges, but at this moment in time we are unable to make a clear statement on the precise nature of the formula of the complex. We did, however, calculate its molar absorption coefficient (MAC), since a 0.02 M copper solution had an absorption max. of 0.64:

0.02 M complex gave 0.64 absorbance in 1 cm path

1 M complex gives 0.64/0.02 absorbance in 1 cm path

$$MAC = 32 \ M^{-1} \ cm^{-1}$$

Pharmaceutical preservatives 28

This exercise is of the same type as the preceding one but there is one important difference. This and the following exercise use genuine pieces of student work, which were shown to us by science teachers as examples of how scientifically quite able students let themselves down when they start to write. We have found them valuable because students often claim that they never make the sorts of mistakes which we invented in exercises 27, 31 and 32 and also that their science teachers are only interested in the content of their written work and not its presentation.

How to run the exercise

a Make copies of the extract about pharmaceutical preservatives, the version without the superscripts.

b Hand these round to the group and ask them in turn to spot a mistake.

c When all the errors have been identified ask the group to rewrite the piece as far as the question 'How should the formulation be tested?' (This includes the sections which need considerable restructuring; after this there is little to be gained from completely rewriting.)

Getting the most out of the exercise

The superscripts identify the major errors which we have picked out for special comment.

Pharmaceutical preservatives

Work in the 1960s greatly[1] brought the problem of inadeuqate[2] presentation 3, 4, 5, 6 [3] to light and much serious thought was given to the problem of microbial contamination. New focus was brought to bear[4] and many new antimicrobials were tested, a few gaining commercial success (7) as pharmaceutical preservatices[5].

The basic[6] properties[7] of any preservative are[8] :

a   It must be physically and chemically compatible with the formulation.

b   Preservatives by their very nature are toxic substances. They must however have minimal toxicity, and cause minimal irritation and sensitisation at the concentrations used.

c   It must be stable under storage.

d   It should have wide antimicrobial activity particularly against the likely contaminants of the particular formulation.

e   Its antimicrobial activity within the laboratory must be tested[9].

It is the last property[10] with which this paper will be concerned. How should the formulation be tested?

There are a number of test structures[11] which have been proposed for measuring the efficacy of preservatives[12]. They are significantly different from the simple tests made directly on preservatives (e.g. minimum inhibitory concentration tests, and kill time[13] experiments). Though these can be useful for making the initial choice of a preservative[14.] They will have little bearing on how the preservative performs within the formulation.

Notes

1 Style.

2 This piece of work was typed by the student who wrote it, but poor typing skills do not excuse errors any more than illegible handwriting or spelling mistakes can be ignored. It is important for students to realise that they will be judged by what they produce (especially if their examiners mark anonymous papers) and that while retyping was not necessary here corrections should have been pencilled in.

3 '3,4,5,6' represent references to a numbered bibliography and should have been isolated from the text in some way, as was done with (7) at the end of the paragraph, to avoid confusion.

4 A classic example of a mixed metaphor.

5 See 2 above.

6 Beware of the word 'basic', which has a precise chemical meaning not applicable here.

7 The phrase 'properties of' seems less suitable for this list than 'requirements for'.

8 Lists are often a problem. If one does not use a full stop at the end of the introductory statement then the whole list should run on grammatically as if it were part of a single sentence, even though the items in the list have been displayed one below the other. This also implies the absence c capitals at the beginning of each listed statement, which perhaps looks rather odd. For

115

example this list could begin

The fundamental requirements for any preservative are

a   physical and chemical compatibility with the formulation;

b   minimal toxicity (though preservatives are by their very nature toxic substances) etc;

Note that the colon is not necessary since it would have no place in the sentence if the list did follow on along the same line. An alternative way of presenting the list, if one wanted to write the requirements as complete sentences, would be to make the introductory statement into a complete sentence. For example

The following list gives the fundamental requirements for any preservative.

a   It must be physically and chemically compatible with the formulation. etc.

Lack of compatibility between the opening statement and the way that the requirements are listed continues throughout points a - d.

9   This is not a required property of a preservative but a requirement of its selection process. Either the author means 'Its antimicrobial activity must be testable within the laboratory' or it should be removed from the list and written as a separate piece of information.

10   See 9 above.

11   Structured tests (?)

12   Add 'within the formulation' (?) to emphasise the distinction which is being made between preservatives on their own (subject to simple tests) and preservatives within the formulation (subject to 'structured' tests).

13   'kill time' (presumably some measure of the time it takes to kill any contaminating organisms) is a piece of invented jargon and must be replaced by a clearer description of the experiments implied.

14   This is not a sentence.

Devising your own materials

Obviously the most valuable material for this sort of exercise will be that provided by the science staff on your own course. Ask them.

Pharmaceutical preservatives

Work in the 1960s greatly brought the problem of inadeuqate presentation 3, 4, 5, 6 to light and much serious thought was given to the problem of microbial contamination. New focus was brought to bear and many new antimicrobials were tested, a few gaining commercial success (7) as pharmaceutical preservatices.

The basic properties of any preservative are :

a   It must be physically and chemically compatible with the formulation.

b   Preservatives by their very nature are toxic substances. They must however have minimal toxicity, and cause minimal irritation and sensitisation at the concentrations used.

c   It must be stable under storage.

d   It should have wide antimicrobial activity particularly against the likely contaminants of the particular formulation.

e   Its antimicrobial activity within the laboratory must be tested.

It is the last property with which this paper will be concerned. How should the formulation be tested?

There are a number of test structures which have been proposed for measuring the efficacy of preservatives. They are significantly different from the simple tests made directly on preservatives (e.g. minimum inhibitory concentration tests, and kill time experiments). Though these can be useful for making the initial choice of a preservative. They will have little bearing on how the preservative performs within the formulation.

What protein is not

Like the preceding exercise this one uses an extract from a genuine piece of student work, selected by a member of the science staff. If you can acquire similar material, critically marked by the staff who teach your students, you can counter the hopeful student claim that no-one minds so long as the science is O K.

How to run the exercise

a   Make copies of the extract about digestion of proteins, the version without the superscripts.

b   Hand these round to the group, asking them to read them carefully and note the places where they think that improvements could be made.

c   Go through the piece from the beginning and ask the group to call out when they want to make a change, discussing the problems and solutions as you go along.

Getting the most out of the exercise

You may like to use the following notes and 'better' version to help you when improving this piece of writing. The notes (which refer to the superscipts in the original) were suggested by the biology teacher for whom this essay was originally written.

The digestion of protein

Protein is not[1] a chemical stimulator of saliva[2], as there is no enzyme in saliva that digests protein - the saliva therefore[3] acts only[4] as a lubricative function[5]. The food is ground into a bolus that is mixed with saliva[6] and swallowed by a voluntary action - when in the oesophagus it is purely involuntary reflex actions taking place[7]. The bolus enters the stomach where further digestion of Carbohydrates[8] and initial digestion of proteins takes place[9]. The gastric glands in the wall of the stomach act as the digestive organs[10] pouring gastric juice into the stomach that contains[11] the digestive enzyme precursors e.g.[12] in this case pepsinogen that is a proteolytic enzyme, i.e.[13] it catalyses the reaction by which proteins are reduced[14] to smaller molecules such as peptones and proteoses.

Notes

1 The essay is about protein digestion and it is unfortunate that it begins with a statement about where protein is *not* digested.

2 When stimulation does occur it is the glands which are stimulated not the saliva, which they produce.

3 Nothing has been said which warrants a 'therefore'.

4 Saliva has other functions; it is just that with protein it functions only as a lubricant. Idiomatically, too, the sentence is faulty: the idiom is 'saliva acts as a lubricant' or 'saliva has a lubricative function'.

5 See 4 above.

6 It is the mixing with saliva which forms the bolus.

7 The first two-thirds of the oesophagus contain voluntary muscles. The sentence is very clumsy.

8 No capital is needed for 'carbohydrates'.

9 'takes' should be 'take', but the whole sentence is better rewritten.

10 The gastric glands *are* the digestive organs.

11 This reads as though there is another stomach somewhere that does not contain the digestive enzyme precursor.

12 'e.g.' is inappropriate as pepsinogen is the only proteolytic enzyme precursor produced in the gastric juice.

13 'i.e.' = that is, so the repetition is unfortunate, but the whole section would be better rewritten.

14 'Reduction' has a specific chemical meaning (not involved in the reaction mentioned here) so avoid in any context where it could be ambiguous.

The digestion of protein ('better' version)

Protein is not a chemical stimulator of salivary glands and there is no enzyme in saliva which digests protein; the saliva acts as a lubricant. The food is ground, mixed with saliva to form a bolus and swallowed by a voluntary action. As it passes down the oesophagus involuntary reflexes take over its movement. The bolus enters the stomach where digestion of carbohydrates continues and protein digestion begins. The gastric glands in the wall of the stomach are the digestive organs, producing gastric juice containing the digestive enzyme precursor, pepsinogen. This gives rise to a proteolytic enzyme, pepsin, which catalyses the conversion of proteins to smaller molecules such as peptones and proteoses.

The digestion of protein

Protein is not a chemical stimulator of saliva, as there is no enzyme in saliva that digests protein - the saliva therefore acts only as a lubricative function. The food is ground into a bolus that is mixed with saliva and swallowed by a voluntary action - when in the oesophagus it is purely involuntary reflex actions taking place. The bolus enters the stomach where further digestion of Carbohydrates and initial digestion of proteins takes place. The gastric glands in the wall of the stomach act as the digestive organs pouring gastric juice into the stomach that contains the digestive enzyme precursors e.g. in this case pepsinogen that is a proteolytic enzyme, i.e. it catalyses the reaction by which proteins are reduced to smaller molecules such as peptones and proteoses.

WRITING UP PRACTICALS
(exercises 30 - 33)

During any science course students will have to write up their laboratory work, and these records may vary considerably in style and detail. Sometimes a class may only be asked to add a series of measurements to a recipe of instructions already prepared by the science staff, at other times a complete practical report in the style of a journal article may be required for assessment (see the section, Report Writing). It is, therefore, important for all students to discover what kind of presentation is preferred by a particular teacher and the first exercise of this section helps them to do this (see also exercise 45).

If students are used to receiving a detailed set of instructions for their practicals they may have little experience in writing these up as Materials and Methods. They may be unsure of how much detail to include and how their material should be divided among the other sections of the report. These problems are dealt with in exercises 31 and 32.

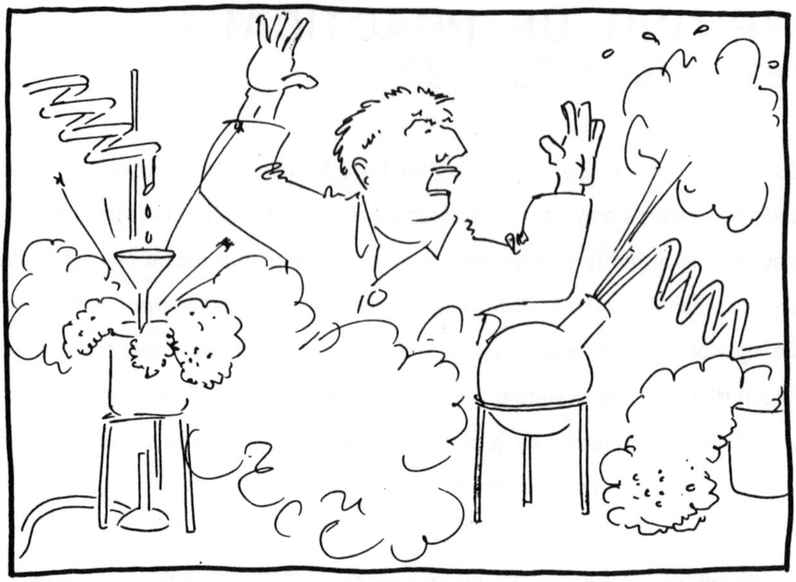

Quick — what do you want to know about this?

Practicals questionnaire 30

If you want to help students to benefit from their practical classes, you will need to find out what the problems and difficulties are and how these are perceived by students and teachers. A simple way of discovering this is to devise a questionnaire for both students and staff to complete.

How to run the exercise

a   Send a copy of the staff questionnaire to everyone who teaches a practical class.

b   Set aside a part of your class time for the students to fill in their questionnaire; not only will this ensure that all students (except for absentees) complete it, it will also give the opportunity for a useful discussion on practicals.

Getting the most out of the exercise

a   The advice which students give on the questionnaire, ostensibly for other students, is advice which they could usefully heed themselves. You can help them by pointing this out and encouraging them to reflect on it and put it into practice.

b   If you organise the questionnaires in such a way that you receive the responses from the staff in time, you can take them along to the questionnaire session with the students. Get the students to fill in their questionnaires first and then show them the responses of the staff for comparison. Students find it very helpful to discover the different requirements of different teachers and the difference between these and their own expectations.

Devising your own materials

a The sample questionnaires consist of open-ended questions. If you want results from your questionnaires in the form of figures, you will need to ask closed questions, e.g. 'Which of the following criteria are used to assess students in practicals?'

b You may prefer to ask your students to devise their own questionnaire rather than give them one ready made. This will ensure that they get the answers to the questions which they think are important rather than those which you have chosen. It will also give them valuable experience in questionnaire design.

Practicals

Dear...............................

As part of my communication courses for science students, I plan to include sessions on practicals. If you have any suggestions as to what I could usefully cover, I would be very glad to see them. The questions below indicate my areas of interest. I would be grateful if you would write your responses and any other comments overleaf.

If you can return this to me by ...., it will give me time to make my preparations.

Thank you very much.

Yours sincerely

....

Q1   What are the main difficulties that students have in practicals?

Q2   What advice should I give students about practicals?

Practicals   -   Questions for students

1   What have you been told are the criteria for assessing students in
     practicals?

2   What other criteria may there be that you haven't been told?

3   What problems do students have in practicals?

4   What advice would you give to next year's students?

Course...Year.............Date...................................

What happened to the gelatin plugs

Because writing up practicals is such an important part of science students' work, the opportunity to practise the necessary skills is very valuable to them. This exercise and the one that follows give students that opportunity. They are also fun.

This exercise consists of two versions of a practical report. One version shows the kind of report you would like your students to be able to produce. The other is based on this model version and includes all the same factual information but has been rewritten with a number of deliberate mistakes, some obvious and some more subtle. The students' task is to correct the errors and rewrite the report in an acceptable form.

This type of exercise has the attraction of a puzzle: students work at it because they are motivated to try and unravel the information. It also makes a point about the conventions of scientific writing because, when they start working on the bad version, students can see for themselves that the style is inappropriate and the format is confusing.

How to run the exercise

a   Give students copies of the bad version and explain the exercise to them. You could say: 'This is a practical write-up which has got quite a few things wrong with it . For instance, you can see straight away that it's written all in one block without any subheadings. Your job is to correct the mistakes and produce a well written report. All the factual information you need is included in this version. Remember to pay attention to details like units as well as language and presentation'.

b When they have done this, give them copies of the model version to compare with what they have written.

c This can lead to a general discussion of the conventions of writing up practicals and also, perhaps, to a critique of the model version.

Devising your own materials

This exercise was written for histology students. Exercise 32 offers a version for food microbiology students. These are complete and ready to use but, if your students are not studying histology or food microbiology, you would be well advised to write your own versions for your own students.

Your model can be the report on a practical which students have done or an alternative to one they have done or a simple practical which they will be doing later in the course. It can be written by a science teacher but it's probably better to use a report written by one of last year's students: the standard will be such that this year's students will feel that they could achieve it.

If you teach science yourself you can keep copies of some of the best of this year's work to use as the basis for such exercises next year. If you have parallel groups you can use the best work of one group in an exercise for the other.

If you don't teach science yourself, writing one of these exercises need present no difficulties: the skills being taught are those of language and presentation rather than content. A science colleague will be able to help you with materials and also tell you about the kinds of error that students on that course commonly make in writing up their practicals.

Wednesday

What happened to the gelatin plugs

When we came into the lab we found some absolute alcohol and some saturated mercuric chloride and some glacial acetic acid and some formaldehyde (10%) and some potassium dichromate (one and a half per cent) and, last but not least, some saturated aqueous picric acid (these are called primary fixatives) and we poured these onto gelatin cork bores which we had first taken from 10% gelatin solidified in Petrie dishes and measured and put into test tubes but we only filled the test tubes half full. (Petri dishes are named after the man who discovered them. He died in 1921.) Then we left it to see what would happen. When we came back on Friday we noticed that the plugs, which were 8m across and 2m thick before, had changed and the plug in the absolute alcohol was entire and white and hardened and measured 5 x 2 and the one in the saturated mercuric chloride was ditto and ditto and 7 x 2 and the one in the glacial acetic acid was almost dissolved and clear and hadn't hardened and was 2 x $\frac{1}{2}$ and the one in the formaldehyde was entire and clear and hardened and 12 x 4 and the one in the p.d. was entire and sticking to the bottom of the tube and orange and hardened and 6 x 1 and the one in the SAPA was ditto but yellow with little or no hardening and 2 x 0.5. All the primary fixatives did different things to the gelatin plugs. Our lecturer said the ones that were bigger or smaller or hardened were the most important ones. The ones that made them harder were absolute alcohol, s.m.c., formaldyhide and potassium dichromate. This is a good thing because this is what fixatives are supposed to be for, isn't it? Absolute alcohol, patassium dichromate and saturated picric acid made the plug shrink a lot; saturated mercuric chloride made it shrink a bit; formaldehyde made it swell. 10% formaldehyde is obviously the best fixative of all. (I'm not sure about glacial acetic acid.)

p.s. I used John and Sarah's results because mine didn't come out right.

Report No. ....

Date ....

An investigation into the effects of six primary fixatives on gelatin plugs

Materials and Methods

Six plugs were taken, using a cork bore, from 10% gelatin solidified in petri dishes and their dimensions were measured. One plug was placed in each of six test tubes. Each test tube was half filled with one of the following primary fixatives:

absolute alcohol

saturated mercuric chloride

glacial acetic acid

formaldehyde (10%)

potassium dichromate (1.5%)

saturated aqueous picric acid

The test tubes were left for 48 hours.

Results

The gelatin plugs initially measured 8 mm in diameter and 2 mm in depth. Gelatin is a proteinaceous derivative of collagen.

Observations on gelatin plugs after 48 h in different fixatives

FIXATIVE	CONDITION	COLOUR	HARDENING	SIZE (mm)
absolute alcohol	entire	white	hardened	5 x 2
saturated mercuric chloride	entire	white	hardened	7 x 2
glacial acetic acid	almost dissolved	clear	no hardening	2 x 0.5
formaldehyde 10%	entire	clear	hardened	10 x 4
potassium dichromate 1.5%	entire: adhering to bottom of tube	orange	hardened	6 x 1
saturated aq. picric acid	entire: adhering to bottom of tube	yellow	no/little hardening	2 x 0.5

Discussion

The different primary fixatives were found to have different effects on the gelatin plugs. Of particular importance are those effects related to shrinkage/swelling (alteration of plug size) and also to hardening of the plug.

Hardening of the plug was achieved by absolute alcohol, saturated mercuric chloride, formaldehyde and potassium dichromate. This is a necessary and desirable effect of a fixative, since hardening enables tissue to be handled more easily and it also safeguards tissue against the damaging effects of subsequent processing.

Alteration of plug size is obviously less desirable since the aim of a fixative is to preserve tissue in as 'life-like' a state as possible. Absolute alcohol, potassium dichromate and saturated aqueous picric acid were found to produce excessive shrinkage of the gelatin plug; saturated mercuric chloride caused slight shrinkage; formaldehyde caused slight swelling. In this context 10% formaldehyde would appear to be the best primary fixative of the six investigated. (Glacial acetic acid appeared to dissolve the gelatin plug and hence its swelling/shrinkage characteristics were difficult to ascertain.)

Milk practical 32

This is the second of two exercises which give students practice in writing up practicals. It consists of two versions of a practical report. One version shows the kind of report you would like your students to be able to produce. The other is based on this model version and includes all the same factual information but has been rewritten with a number of deliberate mistakes, some obvious and some more subtle. The students' task is to correct the errors and rewrite the report in an acceptable form.

How to run the exercise

a   Give students copies of the bad version and explain the exercise to them. You could say: 'This is a practical write-up which has got quite a few things wrong with it. For instance, you can see straight away that it's written all in one block without any subheadings. Your job is to correct the mistakes and produce a well written report. All the factual information you need is included in this version. Remember to pay attention to details like units as well as language and presentation'.

b   When they have done this, give them copies of the model version to compare with what they have written.

c   This can lead to a general discussion of the conventions of writing up practicals and also, perhaps, to a critique of the model version.

Devising your own materials

This exercise was written for food microbiology students. Exercise 31 offers a version for histology students. These are complete and ready to use but, if your students are not studying food microbiology or histology, you would be well advised to write your own versions for the courses which they are following.

Milk practical

It is important that the milk has just been pasteurised and put in the fridge at 2 degrees, give or take half a degree. Three hours later we mixed bits of the milk sample with $1/4$ Wringers (so some mixtures were stronger than others) and made matching sets of plates with YEMA (Yeast Extract Milk Agar). Putting two of each mixture at different tempretures for different numbers of days or hours, at 5^0 until a week later (26th November) at 25 for 2 days and at 37 overnight. There were six plates in the fridge but 3 of the ones in the heated incubators got lost. We counted the colonies and there were different numbers on different plates. We worked out that there were 1×10^4 on the six plates from the fridge and 2×10^5 on the four plates at 25 and 6×10^4 on the five plates at 37. I realised that there were more bacteria in some of the samples than 3×10^4 which is what is allowed in Parsteurised milk. This means that the Pasteurisation Paraflow unit wasn't working properly. Somebody should do something about it.

I thought this was a very interesting experiment. It makes you think, doesn't it?

Report No.................
Date...........................

Routine examination of pasteurised milk sample for total bacterial load

Summary

The sample of pasteurised milk was examined for total bacterial load. The results indicated that the levels were above those recommended as being readily attainable in pasteurised milk: 3×10^4 colony-forming units (cfu)/ml. The Pasteurisation Paraflow unit was recommended for immediate servicing.

Materials and Methods

The milk sample was collected immediately after pasteurisation, and refrigerated (2.0 ± 0.5^0 C) for 3 hours. Appropriate dilutions of the sample were prepared in $^1/_4$ strength Ringer's solution, and replicate pour plates were made using yeast extract milk agar (YEMA). Duplicate plates of each dilution were incubated at 5^0 C for 7 days, 25^0 C for 48 hours and 37^0 C for 24 hours.

Results

Bacterial load of pasteurised milk plated on YEMA at three temperatures

Temperature of incubation (^{0}C)	Bacterial load (cfu/ml)	Number of plates counted
5	1×10^4	6
25	2×10^5	4
37	6×10^4	5

Conclusions and Recommendations

The total bacterial load at the higher temperatures of incubation was greater than the recommended levels (3×10^4 cfu/ml). This indicated inadequate pasteurisation. It was recommended that the Pasteurisation Paraflow unit be serviced immediately.

My experiment failed 33

Probably because a large proportion of a student's practical work may comprise demonstration of known phenomena rather than genuine experiments (see exercise 7) one is frequently confronted by worried students who claim 'I can't write up my practical - it didn't work'. The following is an exercise designed to handle this situation when it arises. It is best used in a one-to-one tutorial.

How to run the exercise

a   Ask the student: 'Were you attempting a practical where an initial hypothesis was tested by an experiment, with results from which conclusions could be drawn, or were you demonstrating or measuring a known effect?'

b   If it was a *demonstration* ask her whether the purpose of the practical was to make measurements on which she must base calculations. In other words was the aim of the exercise to give her practice in data handling? If so then, yes, it is probably helpful for her to borrow someone else's 'successful' results and use them for her calculations. (This is probably what she wants to do anyway.) You might remind her that she must not take credit for the results she is using.

c   If the exercise was merely to demonstrate an effect then it will, of course, help her to understand the subject if she writes a brief account of what she 'ought' to have seen and the theory behind it.

d   Now comes the interesting part. You could start by saying 'You know, you are really *lucky* . Most science teachers judge a report largely on its discussion section and you actually have something to discuss! Instead of demonstrating the predictable, your results were unexpected; now you can write about why this happened'.

e   If the practical was designed as a true *experiment* then the first thing to discover is whether the results unequivocally disproved the hypothesis. If so, then the experiment clearly *succeeded* and the student need only follow scientific method to complete her practical report: in her discussion she should suggest a new hypothesis and propose a suitable experiment to test it.

f   If the results are equivocal or too few for confidence then, yes, the experiment can be said to have failed but the discussion of why this happened can be fascinating (see point d above) :

Were the temperature, pH, circuitry etc. correct?

Was the apparatus in proper working order?

Were enough measurements made?

Were there suitable controls?

Could there have been contamination? How?

Did you have enough time?

How would you do this experiment differently next time?

What further tests would you now like to make?

REPORT WRITING
(exercises 34 - 38)

Laboratory practical accounts are only one particular kind of factual report and it is helpful to demonstrate how rules learned in the context of laboratory experiments extend to any subject where conclusions are drawn from presented evidence. Materials and Methods may well be replaced by an alternative heading: Data Collection or Survey Techniques, for example, and Conclusions may be followed. by Recommendations for Future Action but the underlying principles are the same.

It is useful for students to learn this in a wider context than the laboratory not only because it will relate more closely to their experience outside college but also because it gives them a broader perspective when they plan the structure of their more complicated laboratory practicals.

So Rachel, all we have to do is assess the Sizewell B data, extract the salient points, order them in a logical sequence and conclude with some recommendations for action.

Characteristics of scientific papers

34

The most complete presentation of scientific investigations can be found in the research journals and at some stage most science students will have to present a report in this form. It is a good idea, therefore, to go through one or two research papers with your group and identify the most important characteristics of this type of writing.

How to run the exercise

a   Ask the science staff to recommend some appropriate journals, which publish original research papers rather than popular or review articles.

b   Select two or three which differ from each other in some aspect of present-ation while conforming to a good overall scientific style. You will find, for example, that ways of citing references vary considerably.

c   Arrange to borrow sufficient issues of these journals from the library for everyone to be able to look through and compare them. As you are not going to be reading any specific paper it does not matter if everyone has a different issue of the same journal.

d   When everyone has had a chance to look at a copy of each journal you could say: 'Now I want you to pick out what all the papers have in common. For instance, they all have an abstract. What can you say about the way this is used?'

e   As the group makes its observations collect these together on the board until you have assembled a list of the sections required in any research paper

(Abstract, Introduction, Experimental Procedure, Results, Discussion, References), along with the characteristics of their style and the material they contain.

f Suggest that everyone copies down the final list or compiles their own so that they can refer to it when they have to write up their own major practicals.

Getting the most out of the exercise

a As the group discovers differences between journals and within issues you can discuss 'house style', debating whether one style is better than another and pointing out the importance of internal consistency. (A reader wondering why 'oxidised' is spelt 'oxidized' in the next line is not thinking about *what* is being oxidised.)

b It is a good idea to point out the frequent use of subheadings within the various sections of a paper. Students often ask how they should write up a practical in which several different experiments were carried out on the same material or organism. Clear use of subheadings allows the separate experiments to be presented under the same 'umbrella' headings of Experimental Procedure and Results and then discussed together at the end of the paper.

Project report trouble-shooting

35

Most science teachers give their students advice on how to write project reports. If they don't actually produce their own set of 'house rules' for their students, they will recommend existing guidelines published in a relevant journal or text book. Many students, however, find that a description of good practice and a set of instructions aren't enough : they need help in relating the guidelines to their own material.

This exercise works best if it is done at the stage where students have already done the experimental work for their projects and assembled the data and are just beginning to meet problems in structuring and writing their reports.

How to run the exercise

a   Equip yourself with copies of the guidelines recommended for the course which your students are following.

b   Give your students notice of the date on which you are going to do the 'trouble-shooting' session so that they can bring their project notes with them and come prepared to ask questions.

c   Use the guidelines to give the session its structure. For example if they are set out under subheadings - Title, Abstract, Materials and Methods etc - take these sections one at a time in order.

d   For each section, read out the guidelines, elaborate where necessary and then invite the students to raise points.

151

e   You might say, for example (depending on the content of the guidelines): 'Let's look at the section headed Title in the guidelines. What it says here is "A project title should be clear, concise and informative". Well, I can see a problem right away: the words "concise" and "informative" could be seen to contradict each other. Would some of you who feel satisfied with your project titles like to read them out to us? And then some people who are stuck can describe their difficulties. Who'd like to start?'

f   Resist the temptation to try to answer all the students' questions yourself. Encourage the group to discuss each question and in particular encourage the students with problems to try to find their own solutions.

g   Some problems may be raised which neither the students nor you can solve satisfactorily. This is more likely to happen if you are not a scientist yourself. In this case, rather than leaving problems unresolved, you or the students will need to consult a member of the science staff - preferably the one who is to assess the projects - and report back to the group the following week.

Getting the most out of the exercise

You may be able to persuade a member of the science staff to come to the 'trouble-shooting' session and help with the students' problems. You will need to explain the exercise to her beforehand, though, so that she appreciates what is expected of her.

Abstracts 36

Students need to understand the principles of abstracts both as readers and writers: as readers they waste a lot of time if they are not able to use abstracts to read selectively in journals and as writers they can mislead others if they have had no practice in writing abstracts before they come to write project reports.

How to run the exercise

a You will need multiple copies of several short articles from journals. In the case of one set (or two if you prefer) cut off the abstracts and keep them separately in an envelope.

b Distribute copies of one article with its abstract intact. Ask the students to read it and then get them to identify the characteristics of the abstract and how it relates to the article as a whole. They may also like to criticise it and suggest ways in which it could be improved. (You can organise this part of the exercise as an open discussion or you can get students to work in small groups or write notes individually.)

c When you are satisfied that they understand the principles of abstracts, give them the article with the abstract cut off. Ask them to write an abstract for the article, either on their own or in pairs. They can then compare their abstracts with the author's.

Getting the most out of the exercise
The timing of this exercise is very important. Students should be introduced to the use of abstracts at a time when they are going to be able to use their

knowledge. This is likely to be either when you want them to be able to browse through journals unaided or when they are writing up their projects. Or both: this may be an exercise you want to do twice, with different material.

Structuring a report

Science students generally get very little practice in organising written material: their practical write-ups are usually structured for them and even their essays tend to be judged according to factual content rather than presentation of an argument. So when they have to write a project report or technical report of any kind, they have difficulty organising their material, particularly because they have to give so much of their attention to the content.

This exercise, by focussing on headings and subheadings, enables students to concentrate on organising material without being distracted by the content.

The first example is for full-time students and the second is for day-release students.

How to run the exercise
This exercise is probably best set as a written test. It can be used to assess how far students have understood the principles discussed in exercise 34.

Devising your own materials
Any topic will do as subject for this exercise. You know best what is likely to interest your students.

Structuring a report

Q1 There have been complaints at your college about the poor quality of catering in the refectory. The director has asked you to report on the validity of these claims. List the title, headings and subheadings which you would use in your report, adding brief notes where necessary.

Q2 Your boss has asked you to investigate safety at work and write a report recommending improvements. List the title, headings and subheadings which you would use in your report, adding brief notes where necessary.

The perchloric acid file 38

This exercise is quite a marathon as students are required to confront complicated data, extract only what is relevant and present it in a form that is accessible to various readers with the aim of convincing those readers that they agree with the conclusions of the report. It should test every aspect of report writing and we have, in fact , used it as a major item of assessment.

We have also used The Perchloric Acid File particularly to demonstrate the need for logical order when presenting the various sections of a factual report.

How to run the exercise

a Tell the group that for this exercise they have to imagine themselves to be a technician in a research laboratory.

b Hand round copies of page P1 of The Perchloric Acid File and ask them to read the account which gives the background to the problem which they will be asked to tackle.

c Explain that they will be asked to write a report of the type described and that you will supply them with the information from which they will select their material.

d Hand round copies of page P2, which briefly describes the situation in the laboratory where the students must imagine themselves to be working. You might mention that all the data are based on a genuine situation which arose some years ago in a university physics department.

e It is now helpful to invite questions and begin a discussion of the information so far. It may well be that a member of the group has had experience of handling perchloric acid and it is probable that all science students will have seen or used a fume cupboard in the state described. It is quite possible that some of the group will claim that no one will take any notice of a 'mere' technician or that it would be easier to go straight to the safety officer or the union representative. If this happens you might say: 'The quality and presentation of your evidence will decide how much attention is paid to your complaint, and your union rep. will want to be sure that there is a case to answer before taking the matter further. In other words, you and the issue are likely to be judged on the quality of your report'. (You may have to invent a safety officer who is uncooperative or on sick leave.)

f   Lead the discussion on to the type of recommendations which are appropriate and hand round page P3 of the data, which is taken from the Morgan and Grundy catalogue, together with the extract from the letter from the firm outlining the cost of installation (P4).

g   These costs imply a minimum bill of £4650 (stainless-steel lining, stainless-steel workbase, no fume scrubber) and a maximum bill of £8030 (poly-propylene lining, Grundy ceram workbase, fume scrubber) and you should now tell the group that they will be asked to decide on the appropriate recommendations, which they must justify by presenting the relevant scientific and circumstantial evidence. (The figures are the 1986/7 prices.)

h   The evidence is included in the remaining data on pages P5 - P8, which you should now give to the group, telling them that these are what the imaginary technician has photocopied from various reference texts. Each student must select, from this mass of information, just those facts and recommendations which justify the purchase of expensive new equipment and/or the introduction of a new code of practice in the laboratory.

i   Talk briefly about the people to whom the report will be presented, identifying the audience and thus the tone, level and material which are appropriate in the report. You could, for instance, invent a finance committee including several scientists without specialised knowledge of perchloric acid, an accountant with no understanding of science and anxious to keep costs low, the safety officer (returned from sick leave), who may need convincing that this work can ever be safe, and a director - possibly a retired rear-admiral. There are endless possibilities here.

j   Now summarise the objectives of the exercise. Each student will be asked to write a report which leads the reader to agree with the conclusions about the necessary course of action. The structure of the report should be as rigorous as any laboratory practical account (paper title, introduction to the problem under investigation, statement of aims, presentation of evidence, conclusions, recommendations). It should use appropriate language (note that the language of our introduction on the first page of the material for this exercise is very casual and, therefore, inappropriate for the report), clear layout and suitable headings.

k   We have found that this exercise works well if spread over two sessions: the first introduces the material, which the students can then take away to assimilate in their own time, and the second allows up to two hours to write the report in class.

Getting the most out of the exercise

a   Some extra information may be useful, particularly if you are a non-scientist.

1   A water wash is a spray system plumbed into the fume cupboard ducting as illustrated in the extract from the catalogue.

2   A fume scrubber, built into the ducting which ventilates the fume cupboard to the outside of the building, is designed to minimise atmospheric pollution. It is very expensive to install and is only needed when much larger quantities of perchloric acid are involved than are being used here.

3   Stainless steel is cheaper than polypropylene and Grundy ceram but the relative merits of the different materials must be assessed. Stainless steel is more heat-resistant than polypropylene and can withstand a naked flame. Is the fume cupboard to be used for high-temperature work? Certain chemicals and acids attack stainless steel quite severely (though it is resistant to perchloric acid) while polypropylene and Grundy ceram will resist most solvents and chemicals. Will the use of the fume cupboard be restricted to perchloric acid experiments?

4   The relevant properties of perchloric acid which make it dangerous are (i) hot 60-70% perchloric acid in water (the concentration in which it is usually supplied) is a powerful oxidising agent which will ignite inflammable materials such as wood; (ii) concentrations above 55% in non-aqueous solutions are explosive and can be detonated by heat; (iii) salts of perchloric acid are explosive and can be detonated with a blow. These properties justify the replacement of a teak and tile fume cupoard.

5   The property of perchloric acid which makes it safe is that solutions less than 85% in water at room temperature are completely stable. This

justifies the water-wash equipment.

b   In assessing the perchloric acid reports which students have written for us we
    have looked for the following sort of structure:

    Title

    Introduction, including a statement of the aims of the report

    Properties of perchloric acid which make it safe

    Properties of perchloric acid which make it dangerous

    Selected recorded accidents

    Situation in the lab in the light of the above evidence

    Recommendations for (i) new equipment (ii) new code of practice

    Conclusions

We have also stressed the importance of systematically listing the references
from which the evidence has been obtained, especially since the writer of the
report may be asked 'How do you know all this?' by a senior member of the
company.   Students often fail to group their material correctly under their
chosen headings.   For example, they may include a statement such as
'perchloric acid should be kept in glass-stoppered bottles' in a list headed
'Properties of perchloric acid'. It is worth bringing out the need for care in this
area and also stressing that it is important to arrange the report in a logical
order.   For instance, no conclusions should be drawn or recommendations
made until the evidence for these has been cited. It is also better that any list
of precautions for safe handling, which a student may wish to include, follows
the order of operations which a user will probably take: personal preparation,
storage of the acid, experimental procedure, spillages.

c   Although the material is very highly specialised this exercise can be run successfully with students who lack laboratory experience if you give them a lot of help in extracting the relevant chemical information. You could also ask a member of the science staff if they have a fume cupboard of the type described (most traditional teaching institutions will have several) which you could set up to look as disgusting as the account suggests, and photograph. This has helped people who have never set foot in a laboratory to do well in this exercise.

d   If any of the class should suggest that it is only necessary to staple the photocopied material together and send a covering letter you might ask them whether they would expect anyone to bother to read their own practical reports if they simply handed in the raw data and a conclusion.

Devising your own materials

One is clearly very fortunate to come across a situation which is ready-made for turning into an exercise of this sort but it is well worth while being on the lookout. Remember that you can always invent a scenario which simplifies or complicates a problem, and it can be fun.

The Perchloric Acid File

Your laboratory possesses two fume cupboards, both traditional custom-built teak efforts with tiled work surfaces, both containing a predictable number of winchesters of acetone, methanol, nitric acid, ether etc., bunsens and tripods, and long-forgotten remnants of past experiments now encrusted on the bottoms of dusty flasks.

Increasingly, however, experiments have involved the use of perchloric acid and you are becoming alarmed, having heard that appalling accidents can occur with this chemical. You mention your concern to your boss, who agrees that some action is necessary and asks you to dig out some more information on the subject. Your findings lead you to decide to write a report on the situation, making recommendations for the future which include the purchase of a new fume cupboard and immediate changes in laboratory practice. This report will form the basis of an approach to the departmental finance committee for considerable financial outlay and must, therefore, present the relevant evidence in the clearest and most logical way.

1 The perchloric acid is used for electropolishing, involving approximately 10-30% perchloric acid solutions in acetic acid, methanol, or ethanol, or a mixture of all three. The quantities are not large. No heating is required - in fact, the process is most effective when solutions are kept cold - but passage of an electric current through these solutions may cause an accidental excessive temperature rise.

2 There is no room for a third fume cupboard; any new one installed would have to replace one of the existing ones, which are heavily used.

3 The old grout around the tiles of the existing fume cupboards is quite porous and will absorb and concentrate spilled chemicals.

4 There is no possibility of 'modernising' the old fume cuboards.

5 Your lab has been directed to keep expenditure to a minimum.

Special Features for Fume Cupboards

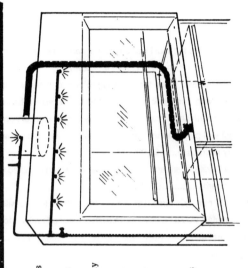

Water Wash

For periodic washing down of the fume cupboard and ducting system before and after, but not during, use. This is essential when the fume cupboard is used for PERCHLORIC ACID. For this duty, each fume cupboard requires its own separate water-washed extract system. Note also that water-wash is incompatible with fire dampers and sound attenuators.

When the water wash is turned on some mist and spray is carried over into the working area and any apparatus or experiments that may be damaged by this should be removed.

When continuous washing of fumes is called for, a fume scrubber must be specified — these are covered in the fume extraction section of this catalogue.

Ventilated Cupboard Understructure

Winchesters of acids are frequently stored in the units under fume cupboards, and to stop any build up of fumes these can be vented directly into the fume cupboard extract system. As additional features, these units are PVC lined and fitted with PVC drip trays.

Special Hazards

The specification of the correct materials within the fume cupboard is necessary for the protection of operating personnel, and long life of the fume cupboard when using specific reagents, etc.

Among the most commonly used are:

Perchloric acid

The hazard with this reagent is that it can form explosive compounds when it comes into contact with organic material. For this reagent the fume cupboard must be lined with either stainless steel or polypropylene, and must be fitted with water wash equipment to wash down any condensed acid. The work surface should be either stainless steel or Grundyceram.

Unit 8, Rainbow Industrial Estate,
Trout Road, Yiewsley, West Drayton, Middx, UB7 7RN.   7th October, 1986

Dear Sirs,

As requested we have enclosed the most up to date version of our data on Perchloric Acid Fume Cupboards (Page 17 within the enclosed brochure).

An indication of the costs involved when tackling the problem of water washing a fume cupboard suitable for use with perchloric acid are listed below, with a base cost for a general purpose fume cupboard and extract system to give further comparison.

1   1500 mm wide general-purpose fume cupboard installed with epoxy powder coated liners and Grundy resin base.......£2,000.00

2   Direct fume extract system with an RN series fume extraction fan sited within 3000 mm of fume cupboard................£1,500.00

3   To convert the 1500 mm wide fume cupboard to one suitable for use with perchloric acid the lining materials would be changed from that specified under 1 to either

      a   Stainless steel with water wash facility for an additional cost of.........£250.00 or alternatively,

      b   Polypropylene with water wash facility for an additional cost of.... .....£350.00

4   The work base would also have to be changed to Grundy ceram and fitted with a rear trough to allow the collection of the residue water from the water wash action possibly up to 20 gallons over a five minute period. The additional cost of the ceramic base and rear trough facility is..£330.00

5   Alternatively the work base could be fabricated from acid resisting grade (EN58J) stainless steel with an integral rear trough. The additional cost of a stainless steel base in lieu of the Grundy Resin is.. £50.00

6   The fume extraction system will also require a water washing facility and this takes place in the form of a series of spray jets at 1000 mm intervals and at all bends including the fan and discharge point. A typical additional cost of this facility for that previously mentioned under 2 would be...£850.00 Nett.

The scrubbers that are used for washing the fumes prior to discharge to atmosphere are reported to be 80-90% efficient and cost in the region of £3,000.00 in addition to the basic fume extract system costing £1,500.00.

Analytical Methods Committee

REPORT PREPARED BY THE METALLIC IMPURITIES IN
ORGANIC MATTER SUB-COMMITTEE

Notes on Perchloric Acid and its Handling in Analytical Work

THE Analytical Methods Committee has received the following report from its Metallic Impurities in Organic Matter Sub-Committee. The Report has been approved by the Analytical Methods Committee and its publication has been authorised by the Council.

REPORT

When the Metallic Impurities in Organic Matter Sub-Committee was re-organised in 1955, it was realised that one of its first duties would be the recommendation of different methods for the destruction of organic matter. It was immediately apparent that the use of perchloric acid is becoming increasingly important, but that it has been neglected in many chemical laboratories owing to common misconceptions about the hazards attendant on its use. Smith[1] has stated, and many chemists agree, that perchloric acid can be used with safety, so long as the user possesses a knowledge of its properties and applies the simple precautions that are appropriate. Much is now known of the properties and the appropriate precautions,

PROPERTIES AND USES OF PERCHLORIC ACID

1. Perchloric acid is completely stable under ordinary storage conditions in concentrations of less than 85 per cent. The concentrations normally supplied are 60 and 72 per cent.

2. The azeotropic mixture with water contains 72·5 per cent. of perchloric acid and boils at 203° C at 760 mm pressure, so that the evaporation of an aqueous solution of perchloric acid can never produce an acid of dangerously high concentration. If, however, metallic salts are present, the mixture should not be evaporated to dryness over an open flame.

3. Perchloric acid vapour and inflammable gases form violently explosive mixtures, and care should be taken to avoid their formation.

4. Hot 60 to 72 per cent. perchloric acid is a powerful oxidising agent and oxidises all forms of organic matter, but it loses its oxidising properties entirely when cooled and diluted with water. The constitution and properties of any material must be taken into consideration before treatment with perchloric acid, whether the material be vegetable or animal matter or a pure chemical. Generally, the speed of the reaction can be readily controlled, but samples containing alcohol, glycerol or other substances that form esters should not be heated with perchloric acid or perchloric acid mixtures, except under previously well tried conditions.

5. When permissible, nitric acid should be present during an oxidation by perchloric acid; if possible it should be added before the perchloric acid and definitely before evaporation to fumes. The effect of nitric acid is to moderate the reaction by oxidising the more reactive components at lower temperatures. It should be remembered, however, that heterocyclic substances containing nitrogen are as a rule not readily oxidised by nitric acid, and the possibility of delayed reactions should not be overlooked; other procedures are necessary for their oxidation.

6. Some inorganic materials, such as hypophosphites and tervalent antimony compounds, also tend to form explosive mixtures with perchloric acid when hot. A large excess of nitric acid should always be present when oxidising inorganic salts.

7. Perchloric acid should not normally be used for oxidising organic materials with which it is highly reactive but immiscible, as the reaction is localised in the zone of contact. It should therefore not be used for oxidising materials containing much fat until any excess of fat has been removed, since local over-heating cannot be controlled and the temperature may rise dangerously. The oxidation of other substances, such as sulphur, is, however, slower and readily controlled.

8. When perchloric acid is used as a dehydrating agent, as, for example, in the determination of silica, with subsequent filtration, the residue must be thoroughly washed with dilute hydrochloric acid before the filter-paper is ignited.

9. The use of a face shield is an advisable precaution when perchloric acid is being used in laboratory procedures.

STORAGE AND HANDLING OF PERCHLORIC ACID

10. Perchloric acid is supplied, and should be stored, in glass-stoppered bottles. To prevent the possibility of trouble in the event of breakage, perchloric acid should be kept apart from organic chemicals and reducing substances, especially alcohol, glycerol and hypophosphites.

Bottles of perchloric acid should *not* be kept on wooden shelves or benches, since acid trapped in the stopper joints spills over to the benches and these may at some future time become heated and ignite. They should stand in glass or porcelain dishes or on ceramic or other non-inflammable and non-absorbent benches, preferably in such a position that the acid can easily be washed away in the event of breakage or spillage.

11. Any acid spilled should be diluted with water. Swabs used to wipe it up should be, if possible, of wool waste or some other non-inflammable material and not of cotton-wool or other cellulose material.

Perchloric acid that has become discoloured should be diluted with water and washed away.

Analytical Methods Committee, *Analyst,* 84, 214-215

The material on the following page, P7, is taken from W.J.McG. Tegart,

The Electrolytic and Chemical Polishing of Metals in Research and Industry, Pergamon Press, Oxford, 1959

(1) Rubber protective equipment should be used in handling the mixtures, and such equipment should be cleaned promptly when it has become contaminated with the acid. Perchloric acid is a strong acid and is very corrosive to the skin.

(2) Perchloric acid should be stored away from all inflammable materials.

(3) Perchloric acid solutions should not be used to polish alloys containing bismuth, as an explosive compound may form in this case.

(4) Perchloric acid solutions should not be used in contact with organic materials, since, if local heating occurs, the danger of a violent explosion is increased. This danger is even greater if iron is present in the solution.

(5) "Bakelite" or "Lucite" mounting materials, and cellulose-buse insulating lacquers and materials should not be used in perchloric acid solutions. However, polyethylene ("Alkathene" or "poly-thene") and polystyrene plastics, ebonite and polyvinyl chloride synthetic rubber can be used without danger.

(6) Care should be taken to keep the temperature of the liquid below 35 to 40°C during mixing of perchloric acid and acetic anhydride (or ethyl alcohol), since much heat is evolved. Previously the recommended procedure was to add acetic anhydride to per-chloric acid, but MEDARD, JACQUET and SARTORIUS [104] now recommend the reverse procedure, i.e. the slow addition of perchloric acid to acetic anhydride. Referring to Fig. 27 it will be seen that this procedure avoids the passage of the composition through the explosive range.

(7) Electrolysis of perchloric acid solutions is accompanied by rapid heating of that portion of the electrolyte in contact with the anode. Cooling and stirring arrangements may be necessary to maintain the temperature of the solution below 35°C to avoid possible combustion or explosion. The electrodes should be placed so that localized heating above 35°C cannot occur either during polishing or during removal of the article for washing.

(8) Provision should be made for adequate ventilation wherever perchloric acid–acetic anhydride mixtures are used, since the acetic anhydride gives off obnoxious fumes, particularly when heated.

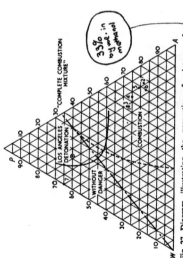

Fig. 27. Diagram illustrating the properties of mixtures of perchloric acid, acetic anhydride and water [104, 105]. The compositions are expressed in wt. per cent and the numbered compositions correspond to the solutions listed in Table 5.

The explosive and combustible properties of perchloric acid solutions can be represented conveniently on the triangular diagram of Fig. 27 [104]. Mixtures containing less than 55 wt. per cent perchloric acid cannot be detonated; these lie in the triangular region below the line joining A to the point on the PW axis corre-sponding to 55 wt. per cent perchloric acid (sp. gr. 1·48). The region to the right of the dotted line in the figure includes compositions which are liable to be inflamed by sparks or general heating. Once combustion begins in these mixtures, it tends to increase in speed and the burning of a large volume of liquid can develop into an explosion. The compositions of mixtures which are theoretically "safe", from the viewpoints of combustion and explosion, are therefore those in the lower left-hand portion of the diagram.

6.3. PRECAUTIONS TO BE TAKEN WHEN USING PERCHLORIC ACID SOLUTIONS

The following general rules should always be observed when using perchloric acid solutions.

When assessing the minimum requirements to insure safe working conditions the following three questions are of importance.

1. Is the work involving the use of perchloric acid likely to be a continuing rather than an occasional and infrequent commitment?

2. Will the use of perchloric acid be accompanied by any form of heating? (Heat of reaction and frictional heat should not be overlooked in this context.)

3. Is it intended to use perchloric acid more concentrated than the 72% azeotrope?

Should the answer to all these questions be "no," then, in the absence of any other contra-indications, relaxation of the normal standards may be considered. If, however, a positive answer is received to any of these questions the working conditions should conform to the recommended standards. Any deviation from these standards should be made only with the agreement of the departmental safety supervisor.

APPENDIX 1—SOME ACCIDENTS INVOLVING PERCHLORIC ACID

1. Explosions may occur when 72% perchloric acid is used to determine chromium in steel, apparently due to the formation of mixtures of perchloric acid vapor and hydrogen. These vapor mixtures can be exploded by the catalytic action of steel particles.[1]

2. Two workers are reported to have dried 11,000 samples of alkali-washed hydrocarbon gas with magnesium perchlorate over a period of 7 years without accident. However, one sample containing butyl fluoride caused a purple discoloration of the magnesium perchlorate with the subsequent explosion of the latter.[1]

3. A worker using magnesium perchlorate to dry argon reported an explosion and warned that warming and contact with oxidizable substances should be avoided.[1]

4. An explosion was reported when anhydrous magnesium perchlorate used in drying unsaturated hydrocarbons was heated to 220°C.[1]

5. An explosive reaction takes place between perchloric acid and bismuth or certain of its alloys, especially during electrolytic polishing.[1,4]

6. Several explosions reported as having occurred during the determination of potassium as the perchlorate are probably attributable to heating in the presence of concentrated perchloric acid and traces of alcohol. An incident in a French laboratory is typical: an experienced worker in the course of a separation of sodium and potassium removed a platinum crucible containing a few decigrams of material and continued the heating on a small gas flame. An explosion pulverized the crucible, a piece of platinum entering the eye of the chemist.[6]

7. A violent explosion took place in an exhaust duct from a laboratory hood in which perchloric acid solution was being fumed over a gas plate. It blew out windows, bulged the exterior walls, lifted the roof, and extensively damaged equipment and supplies. Some time prior to the explosion, the hood had been used for the analysis of miscellaneous materials. The explosion apparently originated in deposits of perchloric acid and organic material in the hood and duct.[7]

Norman V, Shear, ed., *CRC Handbook of Laboratory Safety,*
The Chemical Rubber Company, Cleveland, 1967

WRITING INSTRUCTIONS
(exercises 39 - 40)

While science students are usually on the receiving end of written instructions some of them may eventually take up jobs which require them to write instructions for other people.

They may have to draft technical manuals to accompany complicated pieces of equipment, write directions for a household gadget or instruct a junior in a practical task.

The two exercises which follow are designed to help a student to see the problem through the eyes of the person using the instructions and thus to avoid the major pitfalls of inappropriate language, illogical order and unhelpful layout. Above all they should discover the value of making clear the objective of the instructions before embarking on the steps which lead there.

Married women's pensions

We are grateful to Tom Vernon, the compiler of *Gobbledegook*[1], for providing us with the material for this exercise, which includes two examples of 'good' answers. Although these are not strictly instructions the exercise demonstrates the need for a logical order and an appropriate presentation when giving information. It is a useful preliminary to exercise 40 since it does not require technical knowledge of a particular piece of equipment.

How to run the exercise

a Give your students copies of the passage (A), which attempts to inform women about their entitlement to the married woman's (flat-rate) retirement pension. (This used to be called the old-age pension.)

b Ask them to rewrite this using more comprehensible language, style or format while still including all the information in the passage.

c Show them copies of the *Gobbledegook* versions (B and C), which could be on a transparency.

Getting the most out of the exercise

When comparing the various answers devised by the class it is a good idea to bear in mind the impact of a table or flow chart on someone not used to seeing information displayed in this way. Check to see that students have written an adequate introduction and an informative title.

1 T. Vernon, *Gobbledegook*, National Consumer Council, London, 1980

A 'The earliest age at which a woman can draw a retirement pension is 60. On her own insurance she can get a pension when she reaches that age, if she has then retired from regular employment. Otherwise she has to wait until she retires or reaches age 65. At age 65 pension can be paid irrespective of retirement. On her husband's insurance, however, she cannot get a pension even though she is over 60, until he has reached age 65 and retired from regular employment, or until he is 70 if he does not retire before reaching that age.'

B

MARRIED WOMAN'S (FLAT RATE) RETIREMENT PENSION		
1. I am under 60	Yes:	NO PENSION
	No:	read Question 2
2. I am claiming	(a) on my own insurance:	read Question 3
	(b) on my husband's insurance:	read Question 5
3. I am under 65	Yes:	read Question 4
	No:	PENSION
4. I am working	Yes:	NO PENSION
	No:	PENSION
5. my husband's age is	(a) less than 65:	NO PENSION
	(b) between 65 and 69:	read Question 6
	(c) 70 or more:	PENSION
6. my husband has retired	Yes:	PENSION
	No:	NO PENSION

C

MARRIED WOMAN'S (FLAT RATE) RETIREMENT PENSION

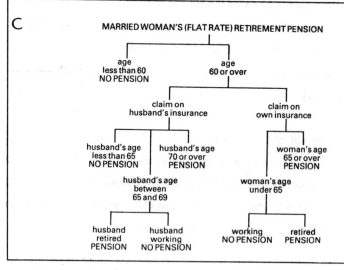

174

Operating instructions 40

This exercise gives students practice in writing instructions for operating pieces of technical or domestic equipment.

How to run the exercise

a   Choose either a piece of laboratory apparatus (pH meter, spectrophotometer, centrifuge, oscilloscope, for example), with which the students are familiar, or a piece of domestic equipment (cooking clock, tin opener) as the subject for this exercise; you could possibly bring it into the classroom.

b   Ask the class to write a set of instructions for using, assembling, servicing or dismantling the equipment, whichever is most appropriate.

c   Ask an inexperienced user (yourself?) to try out some of the instructions in front of the class; that is, if the apparatus is not too delicate.

d   From what they have learned the students then draw up a set of guidelines for writing instructions. They can do this in small groups, who report back to the class, or everyone can contribute to a general brainstorming, afterwards arranging the points in order of importance.

Getting the most out of the exercise

a   In many cases instructions are greatly helped by diagrams but take care that people do not spend too much time perfecting technical drawings instead of completing an outline of the whole project.

b   A variation would be to prepare the class for this exercise at the end of the preceding session by asking them to bring in a piece of equipment with which they are familiar. They would then write the appropriate instructions, exchange these and the apparatus with a neighbour and see how far they can carry out someone else's instructions.

DATA PRESENTATION AND INTERPRETATION
(exercises 41 - 43)

Science students spend a lot of time working with data but in a way which means that they are generally concentrating on implications and calculations rather than giving thought to how data are best communicated.

The exercises in this section encourage students to look at data presentation and interpretation from a critical perspective.

Presenting statistics 41

This is an exercise in appraising the presentation of statistical data. It requires students to be critical of what they read and introduces them to some of the pitfalls involved in handling data.

How to run the exercise
Hand round copies of the exercise and either ask your students for written comments or get them to discuss the passage in class. If you do set it as a test, it is a good idea to have a discussion as well, since there are important principles to be appreciated: the alteration of the statistical sample from Britain to the whole world in paragraph 4, for instance, and the questionable benefits of presenting statistics in this way.

Devising your own materials
Look out for statistical material which is illogically or unhelpfully presented and get your students to criticise it. Or, if you have difficulty finding existing examples, you can produce your own. An easy way to do this is to take a well produced statistical table and alter it to illustrate the kinds of mistakes that students commonly make: you can omit units, for example, or give it an uninformative title or include unnecessary repetition.

The dangers of air travel

Comment on the use of logic and statistical data in the following passage.

Flying is an unnatural act. Just how dangerous is it? Perhaps the question should be: just how safe is it? It is certainly a lot safer than driving your car - for the average driver, allowing for the fact that the average person spends a lot more time driving than flying. Road deaths in the world are around a quarter of a million a year; deaths in airliners between 1,000 and 2,000.

The safest form of transport is rail and the most dangerous the motorbike. Say 100 people travelled for 5,000 miles a year, the average for Europeans. Before one of them could expect to be killed the group would have to travel: by rail, 1,540 years; by bus, 1,000 years; by scheduled air transport, 370 years; by private car, 133 years; by motorcyle, seven years.

Flying carries a risk of dying of one per million hours. This is about the same as that for dying from all causes, which is below one in a million until you're 35 or 40, and then begins to go up, reaching five in one million by 70. Or to put it another way - always helpful with statistics - flying as a passenger today is no more risky than being 55 years old.

Accident rates for non-scheduled flights are higher than those of scheduled airlines. But both are very low. Despite an immense increase in the volume of traffic, air transport in general has been getting safer and safer and the experts predict that it will continue to do so. In 1935 the British figure for fatal accidents per million flights was 67. At the beginning of the 1960s the world rate was about four per million. It is now just below three.

Flow charts 42

Flow charts are widely used to illustrate scientific processes. This exercise gives students practice in drawing them (see also exercises 14 and 47).

How to run the exercise

a Give your students copies of the exercise and ask them to draw a flow chart. Don't worry if you don't understand the technical material they are dealing with: the exercise is about the flow chart as a method of presentation and is not concerned with content.

b Give them some time (about 10 minutes) to work in pairs looking at each other's charts and noting examples of good practice.

c Ask each pair in turn to contribute one example of good practice. These can be listed on the board under the heading 'How to draw a good flow chart'.

Flow charts

Either draw a flow chart to illustrate a process you are familiar with, e.g. a scientific process you have learned about at college or a technical process you have been involved in at work,

or draw a flow chart to illustrate your life so far. Indicate stages in the process and alternatives to the choices which you have made (or which have been made for you) in your life.

Show clearly where your flow chart begins and ends.

Vary the shape of your boxes and the thickness of your arrows according to the message you want to convey.

Choosing a method of presentation

43

Science students are generally familiar with a variety of methods for presenting data and they can draw graphs, histograms and pie charts with ease but they are usually less skilled at choosing between the methods and selecting the best one for the task in hand.

This exercise gives them the opportunity to compare a range of methods and practise making choices between them.

How to run the exercise

a   Give your students a copy of the exercise. While they are drawing, tour the room and look at their work. You will probably find that at least one student has chosen each of the methods (graph, histogram, pie chart) and that some have attempted other pictorial methods.

b   Conduct a review of the different methods, calling on particular students to illustrate them on the board.

c   You can follow this up by giving students a set of more complex scientific data to present.

Getting the most out of the exercise

If you are not familiar with graphs etc. you may find the following notes helpful.

a   Look out for two students who have both drawn graphs but using different scales in such a way that the increase on one looks greater than on the other.

You can use these to show how factual information can be misrepresented.

b The function of the pie chart is to illustrate proportions. Since these figures are not proportions of anything (except their sum) a pie chart is not appropriate here.

c Some students may have attempted the kind of statistical presentation often seen on television and drawn pictures of unemployed people. If so it is important to check how they did their calculations. A picture of a person who is twice the height of another has more that twice the area and so looks more than twice as big (apart from the fact that people are normally three-dimensional).

Various ways of presenting the data: unemployment, UK, 82-87

Choosing a method of presentation

Draw a graph, histogram, pie chart or other pictorial representation of the following data.

Unemployment in the UK

(in thousands)

1982	1983	1984	1985	1986	1987
2,917	3,105	3,160	3,271	3,408	3,297

Employment Gazette, Department of Employment, London, 1987

I used to find tables difficult to design until I asked myself what they are for.

THE ARRANGEMENT OF DATA IN TABLES
(exercises 44 - 46)

Possibly because they are rarely taught the ground rules of table layout, students frequently find tables difficult to design, especially when handling a wide range of information.

Here is a summary of what we think makes a good table, which you may find useful if you have not had much to do with this form of data presentation.

Tables correlate data tidily without revealing the trends or mathematical relationships displayed by graphs.

It is useful to consider a table as being made up of a series of lists or vertical columns, each with its own heading, which are then aligned side by side so that the data correlate horizontally. It should be clear whether a heading applies to information alongside it or below it and in general (there are always exceptions) a heading should apply to the information beneath it not beside it.

A good table is compact and has a minimum number of blank spaces or repetitions. However, if this can only be achieved by an elaborate system of footnotes, colour codings, compressions or words turned sideways, think again. It may show that *you* have understood how it all fits together but your readers may not have the patience to find out whether they agree with you.

Improve this table

44

This exercise offers students practice in criticising and improving the layout of a table. The example given is a table which breaks a few basic rules and can be corrected very simply.

How to run the exercise

a Hand round copies of Table 1 (or use an overhead projector).

b Ask the class for constructive criticism, possibly directing their ideas with questions such as: 'Is the title adequate?' 'What is being measured? Is there a headline above the data stating this?' 'What is varying as a function of what?' 'Do the percentage symbols need to be repeated?'

c Assemble their suggestions into a new version of the table on the lines of Table 2.

Getting the most out of the exercise

In answering the above questions it is probable that someone will suggest turning the table through 90^0, a solution which is worth illustrating fully by showing the class Table 2. It is surprising how often table sorting can seem problematical simply because we are looking at the data the wrong way round.

Devising your own materials

It is easy to find examples of good and bad tables in newspapers, magazines, books and journals and you can, of course, always rearrange a published table to demonstrate the points you want to make.

Improve this table

Table 1. V and K_m values

Glutaraldehyde mM	0	0.125	0.25	0.5	0.75	1
Residual V	100%	100%	98%	69%	55%	48%
K_m mM	0.32	0.39	0.44	0.55	0.65	1

Table 2.   The variation of V and K_m values of phosphofructokinase as a function of increasing glutaraldehyde concentration

Glutaraldehyde concentration	V	K_m
mM	%	mM
0	100	0.32
0.125	100	0.39
0.25	98	0.44
0.5	69	0.55
0.75	55	0.65
1	48	1

Is this how you will do it? 45

This exercise in table layout is more complex than exercise 44. It is an account of a histology practical written by a former student.

How to run the exercise

After handing round copies of 'Fixation and its effect on staining', ask for constructive criticism, prompting the discussion with questions and suggestions such as those outlined in a - f below.

a   What is the aim of displaying data? [To organise the information so that you are best able to make connections and draw conclusions.]

b   What connections are you required to make in this experiment? [Compare three fixatives in terms of

   1   their effect on the tissue;

   2   their effect on the efficiency of subsequent staining.]

c   How could the student who wrote this account have made these comparisons more effectively?

   [1   By using the same language to describe the effects, e.g. urinary space is described as both 'medium' and 'average'. Is there a difference? Is 'dark blue' different from 'intense blue'? Is it worth considering a +, ++, +++ code for recording qualitative data in tables?

   2   By avoiding unnecessary repetition of words common to a whole group of observations in the table, e.g. 'blue' in the column describing the nucleus.

   3   By combining the results into a single table, or does this make the shape too unwieldy?

4 By stating precisely what is being recorded in each column, e.g. not 'RBCs' but 'condition of RBCs'.

5 By recording the different fixatives in the same order in the two tables.

6 By giving the tables an adequate title.]

d Are the abbreviations helpful or a distraction? [Spatial factors often make them necessary in tables though they should be discouraged in the main text. If abbreviations are used they must be defined.]

e What is successful in these tables? [The author has helpfully grouped her observations illustrating the two aspects under investigation - effects on staining and effects on the tissue - at opposite sides of the tables.]

f Table A is a version of these tables, which attempts to incorporate some of your suggestions. What do you think of it?

Getting the most out of the exercise

One of the best ways of guaranteeing the interest of students in an exercise of this sort is to use an experiment which they have just performed and are about to write up.

If the class are first-year students at the beginning of their course this can also be a valuable way of showing them just what sort of practical account is expected by a particular teacher. After handing out copies of the chosen practical account to the class you might say, for example, 'The quantity and quality of the information in this student's work are at the level required by Dr H. He told me that he gave this student a B, which would have become A- if diagrams had been included and the tables had been more systematic'.

Devising your own materials

Ask one of the science staff for a sample of the work of a student who has already done the course, if possible gaining the permission of the student herself. It is important that the scientific content of the practical account chosen is of good quality, otherwise the discussion will concentrate on the value of the results and not on the presentation.

Fixation and its effect on staining

Aim: To investigate the effect of three different fixatives on the subsequent staining techniques with H. and E., and Martius-scarlet-blue.

Method: See hand-out sheet.

Results: These are shown in the following table.

	Nucleus	Intensity of eosin	Size urinary
N.B.F	intense blue	not very intense	quite wide
Carnoy	very intense	quite intense pink	wide
F.S.	light blue	not v. intense	not very wide

The above results are those of the fixatives with H. and E. Below are the results with Martius scarlet blue.

	Intensity nucleus	Col. tubule	R.B.C.'s	Size U space
NBF	dark blue	red/orange	good, bright yellow	large
FS	clear outline	red/granular	average, yellow	medium
Carnoy	v.v. dark	bright red	orange	average

Conclusions ...

Table A

The effect of three different fixatives and subsequent staining on rat kidney tissue

Fixative	Effect of staining with haematoxylin + eosin			Effect of staining with Martius scarlet blue			
	nucleus (stains blue)	tubule cytoplasm (stains pink)	size of urinary space	nucleus (stains blue)	tubule cytoplasm	cond'n of red blood cells	size of urinary space
Neutral buffered formalin	intense	light	quite wide	intense	red/orange	good, bright yellow	large
Carnoy	very intense	quite intense	wide	v. v. intense	bright red	orange	medium
Formol sublimate	light	light	narrow	clear outline	red/granular	average yellow	medium

The detergent treatment

Many students have difficulty in organising the results of the more open-ended experiments which make up simple research projects, the type of experiment which is more likely to conclude with suggestions about how to do it better next time than with a 'right' answer. These experiments, valuable because they require the student to think for herself, often have to be correlated with the results of other groups in the class, and the presentation of data gleaned from different people, different apparatus and at different times can be a formidable problem.

This exercise attempts to simulate this situation. It requires the student to organise data by reasoned sorting and common sense and present them as a coherent table of sensible proportions. We have found that it works well with students studying any of the sciences as it requires an ability to organise information logically rather than an understanding of the subject matter of the table.

How to run the exercise

a   Hand round details of the exercise and allow five minutes for the class to read them through and discuss them.

b   When any questions have been answered suggest that everyone decides what is the *purpose* of the table. What is being observed as a function of what main variable?

c   Allow the class 30 minutes to devise the table. Students often do this exercise best in pairs.

d   Groups who have solved the problem in very different ways can be asked to present their solutions to the class. If everyone has been asked to sketch their final efforts on transparencies an overhead projector can be used for the presentations.

e   Ask the class to discuss the relative merits of the various solutions.

Getting the most out of the exercise

If a class appears to be getting nowhere suggest that they make a few preliminary notes by asking themselves what the variables are [reactions: E1, E2; detergents: nine different ones; quinones: Q-2, Q-10; assays: A,B,C,D,E]

Then they can try a few correlations such as

1   E1 uses Q-10 and Q-2
    E2 uses Q-10 and Q-2

2   Q-10 is investigated with two detergents
    Q-2 is investigated with eight detergents

3   Q-10 is assayed by methods A,D,E,B,C
    Q-2 is assayed by methods A,B,D,E

4   E1 is assayed by methods A,B
    E2 is assayed by methods C,D,E

Points 2 and 4 suggest simplifications in what may appear a bewildering mass of unconnected data.

A decent, though not definitive, version of the final table might look like the one shown below, which is arrived at by the following steps.

1   What is the purpose of the table? To record reaction velocities as a function of detergent type, so the layout begins thus

        Detergent   Velocity of reaction

2   How many reactions? Two: E1, E2, hence

Detergent	Velocity of reaction	
	E1	E2

3   What do we know about the distribution of assay systems used? E1 uses A, B; E2 uses C, D, E, so we get

Detergent	Velocity of reaction				
	E1 assayed by		E2 assayed by		
	A	B	C	D	E

4   What have we omitted? Quinone type and units, which gives the following completed table.

Detergent	Quinone	Velocity of reaction (U)				
		E1 assayed by		E2 assayed by		
		A	B	C	D	E
Triton X-100	Q-10	2000	400	1300	500	400
Octyl glucoside	Q-10	2200	-	-	-	-
Triton X-100	Q-2	2300	600	-	800	700
Triton X-165	Q-2	2200	1300	-	1100	1100
Emulphogen	Q-2	2100	300	-	200	200
Brij 35	Q-2	2100	2000	-	1100	1000
Brij 56	Q-2	2300	700	-	300	400
Brij 58	Q-2	2100	1000	-	600	600
Tween 20	Q-2	2400	1000	-	900	1000
Tween 80	Q-2	2300	1000	-	800	800

The detergent treatment

The following results are based on those published by Weiss and Wingfield[1]. Experiments were carried out to investigate the effect of detergents on two oxidation/reduction reactions. (These reactions take place in living cells and are carried out by enzyme systems which are frequently bound to fatty tissue in the cell membranes. Detergents will release the enzymes from the membranes and are used in investigating the mechanism of their catalytic activity.)

The reactions under investigation may be represented by the following equations:

$$XH_2 + Q = X + QH_2 \qquad \text{(reaction E1)}$$
$$QH_2 + Y = Q + YH_2 \qquad \text{(reaction E2)}$$

Q stands for a quinone derivative (ubiquinone) and two types of ubiquinone were used in the reactions: Q-2 and Q-10.

The effects of nine different detergents were investigated, identified mostly by their trade names: Triton X-100, Triton X-165, octyl glucoside, Emulphogen, Brij 35, Brij 56, Brij 58, Tween 20, Tween 80.

Five different assay systems were used to measure the reaction velocities: A, B, C, D, E.

The reaction velocities were recorded in arbitrary units (U) for comparison between the various systems.

Results

Using assay A with Q-10
for reaction E1

Detergent	Velocity of E1
Triton X-100	2000 U
Octyl glucoside	2200 U

Using assay B with Q-10
for reaction E1

Detergent	Velocity of E1
Triton X-100	400 U

Assay C was only used for reaction E2 with Q-10 and Triton X-100 as the detergent. The result was 1300 U.

Using assay D with Q-10
for reaction E2

Detergent	Velocity of E2
Triton X-100	500 U

Using assay E with Q-10
for reaction E2

Detergent	Velocity of E2
Triton X-100	400 U

Using assay A with Q-2 for
reaction E1 (U)

Detergent	Velocity of E1
Triton X-100	2300
Triton X-165	2200
Emulphogen	2100
Brij 35	2100
Brij 56	2300
Brij 58	2100
Tween 20	2400
Tween 80	2300

Using assay B with Q-2 for
reaction E1 (kU)

Detergent	Velocity of E1
Emulphogen	.03
Tween 20	1
Tween 80	1
Triton X-165	1.3
Triton X-100	0.6
Brij 56	0.7
Brij 58	1
Brij 35	2

Assays D and E gave identical results for reaction E2 when Q-2 was the ubiquinone used with the following detergents:

Detergent	Velocity of E2
Triton X-165	1100 U
Emulphogen	200 U
Brij 58	600 U
Tween 80	800 U

For the remaining detergents assays D and E gave the following results with Q-2 and reaction E2

Assay D

Triton X-100 = 800 U: Brij 35 = 1100 U; Brij 56 = 300 U;
Tween 20 = 900 U

Assay E

Triton X-100 = 700 U; Brij 35 = 1000 U; Brij 56 = 400 U;
Tween 20 = 1000 U

Collect all these results together into a single table, taking care to see that column headings are unambiguous and that no information is duplicated or omitted. When planning your layout, consider what shape you wish your final table to be.

1 H. Weiss and P. Wingfield, *European Journal of Biochemistry*, 99, 151-160, 1979

Well Eric, your non verbal communication is excellent and you sound very enthusiastic, but we were a little worried when you couldn't remember your name.

ORAL PRESENTATIONS
(exercises 47 - 49)

'Some of them can only talk to their computers and not to the rest of us.' We frequently hear this type of criticism from employers, who ask that the teaching of oral skills be included in science-based courses.

We hope that the exercises in this section will help students to give a lively oral presentation, which still obeys all the rules for communicating scientific material.

Using the overhead projector 47

This exercise can serve as an introduction to the techniques of giving presentations. It offers students the opportunity to practise using the overhead projector and also leads them gently into the experience of giving a short presentation.

How to run the exercise

a You will need:

    1 an overhead projector (check beforehand that it's working);

    2 an overhead projection transparency for each student (the flimsy variety is cheaper though if your students take a pride in their work they may prefer the stiff variety which is more durable);

    3 an overhead projector pen for each student (if these are not available, ordinary felt-tip pens will do).

b Give the students instructions along these lines: 'This is an exercise in presenting things visually. What you present can be anything you like: some aspect of your studies, for example, or something to do with one of your other interests. It doesn't really matter what you choose as long as it's something that lends itself to being presented in the form of a chart or a diagram. For instance, you might want to do a flow chart to illustrate a technical process or a plan of the parts of a motor bike or a family tree of the characters in *Dallas*. I think it's a good idea, though, if it's something that the rest of the class is not too familar with because if they are, it'll be likely to be boring for them and also it won't be much of a test of your communication skills. You've got twenty minutes to do this'.

c   At this stage you can be helpful to them by making points about the size of lettering needed on OHP transparencies, and the scope for tracing etc.

d   After twenty minutes you could say, 'Now you will all have a turn at presenting your OHP transparency to the rest of us. When it's your turn, just give a brief explanation of what you've drawn and be prepared to answer our questions'.

e   Make points about positioning oneself in relation to the projector and the screen, pointing at the transparency rather than the screen etc.

Getting the most out of the exercise

a   Nervous students tend to try to rush this exercise: they may display their transparency, say 'This speaks for itself' and sit down again. You can counteract this by encouraging the other students to ask questions.

b   Once students have done this exercise they should have more confidence to use visual aids in the future. They may still need encouraging to use them, though. You could do this by reminding them, by always having transparencies available for them to use and by allocating a proportion of the marks given for presentations to the use of visual aids.

Self and peer appraisal   **48**

Self and peer appraisal is a democratic way of managing learning which gives students the opportunity to develop proficiency in evaluating themselves and others and in giving and receiving feedback. Its application to assessed presentations means that all students are actively involved instead of passively providing an audience for each other's presentations and uncritically accepting the teacher's assessment.

If there are assessed presentations on your courses, this exercise will give you the opportunity to share that assessment with your students.

How to run the exercise
(This is a weekly routine which will need explanation the first time you use it but not subsequently, once the students are familiar with it.)

a   Identify the students who are to give their presentations that week, e.g. Ann and Steve. Divide the remainder of the class into two groups and call them Ann's Support Group and Steve's Support Group.

b   Give all students a copy of a checklist of criteria on which they are to base their appraisal. Ideally this should be a checklist which the students themselves have devised and agreed. If you don't have a chance to do this, you can duplicate the sheets which follow.

c   Explain to the class that, as Ann gives her presentation, the members of her support group should pay special attention to her, according to the checklist criteria, and note down points which will make helpful feedback for her.

Steve's group is to do the same for Steve.

d   After both presentations, get Ann and Steve to join their support groups so that they can receive feedback from them. Advise them to note down helpful points. This will take about 5 - 10 minutes.

(When you introduce this exercise for the first time, you will need to point out to students the value of balancing negative and positive feedback, encouraging them to give constructive criticism as well as specific praise.)

e   If there are not too many constraints on your assessment methods, you can have the support groups also give Ann and Steve a mark.

f   Give Ann and Steve copies of the self-appraisal sheet. Ask them to complete it, using the feedback from their support groups to help them, and hand it in to you the following week. You can take this self-appraisal into account in your assessment, giving credit for a student's sensitivity to the audience, willingness to learn from mistakes etc.

Assessed presentations: criteria for appraisal

1   **Position**

Were the positioning of the audience, visual aids and speaker appropriate?

2   **Voice**

fluent/hesitant?

audible/inaudible?

too fast/too slow?

monotonous/varied?

3   **Content**

interesting?

relevant?

4   **Structure**

logical?

clear to audience?

any repetition?

any under/over emphasising?

5   **Notes**

Was the speaker too dependent on them?

Did they break the relationship between the speaker and the audience?

6 Timing
too long/too short?

7 Eye contact
with everyone in the audience/a few/one/nobody?

8 Visual aids
clear?

attractive?

explained well?

relevant?

9 Answering questions
Were questions answered appropriately?

10 Relationship with audience
Was there a good relationship between the speaker and the audience?

Did the speaker impart enthusiasm?

Now please add overleaf any other comments not covered above which will be helpful to the speaker

Assessed presentations: self-appraisal sheet

by...

1   Thinking of the presentation as a whole, what are the main points
you would make about it?

2   What do you think your audience felt about it?

3   How would you alter your presentation, if at all?

Scientifically speaking 49

It is important that science students should learn how to talk interestingly and logically about their subject, but a scientific talk, presented to students on the same course, does not really test the speaker's ability to convey new information clearly. The speaker may assume that everyone knows all about it already and so not bother to explain things properly or she may feel undermined by the suspicion that some of the audience know more about the subject than she does.

This exercise avoids these problems by requiring each student to speak on a non-scientific subject of their choice using the conventions of a scientific presentation. It thus also tests the student's understanding of the rules governing a communication process without the support of conventional material (see also exercise 6).

How to run the exercise

a   Tell your students that they will each have to give an oral presentation in which they can speak for a maximum of 15 minutes and then answer any questions from the audience.

b   Say that they may choose any topic so long as it is not scientific or technical, but that they must follow the conventions for presenting technical material.

c   Here you could remind them of the criteria for a good scientific report (appropriate language; objectivity; clear statement of the problem/topic under investigation; methods, if appropriate; evidence; discussion; conclusions *based on that evidence*). It is actually quite easy to translate this approach to a non-scientific subject since the principles apply to any factual presentation.

d   Tell the group that they will be assessed on the extent to which their talks conform to these requirements and on the criteria for good oral presentations summarised in the appraisal sheets (which follow).

e   Hand round copies of the instructions for this exercise together with the appraisal sheets. Ask for volunteers to commit themselves to giving the first presentations.

Getting the most out of the exercise

a   There are bound to be questions about the use of visual material and demonstrations and you can tell them about the equipment available (if they have done exercise 47 they will have used the overhead projector already). It is worth warning everyone that they ought to familiarise themselves with the equipment beforehand. We've all discovered how much time can be wasted on focussing, dimming lights and un-jamming slide carousels and that demonstrations often go uniquely wrong when there's an audience.

b   It's a good idea to arrange that not more than two of these presentations are given per session. They demand considerable audience concentration if the speaker is to get as much out of the exercise as possible.

c   This exercise lends itself to self and peer appraisal (exercise 48).

Assessed presentations

1 Topic

Any topic may be chosen except a technical or scientific topic.

2 Treatment

The topic should be presented in the format of a good scientific report.

3 Timing

A maximum of 15 minutes is allowed for the presentation, which should be followed by questions from the audience. There is no minimum time requirement.

4 Criteria for assessment

Marks will be awarded according to item 2 (above) and the criteria on the accompanying sheets.

Students will submit a self-appraisal sheet.

Assessed presentations: criteria for appraisal

1 **Position**

Were the positioning of the audience, visual aids and speaker appropriate?

2 **Voice**

fluent/hesitant?

audible/inaudible?

too fast/too slow?

monotonous/varied?

3 **Content**

interesting?

relevant?

4 **Structure**

logical?

clear to audience?

any repetition?

any under/over emphasising?

5 **Notes**

Was the speaker too dependent on them?

Did they break the relationship between the speaker and the audience?

6   **Timing**

too long/too short?

7   **Eye contact**

with everyone in the audience/a few/one/nobody?

8   **Visual aids**

clear?

attractive?

explained well?

relevant?

9   **Answering questions**

Were questions answered appropriately?

10   **Relationship with audience**

Was there a good relationship between the speaker and the audience?

Did the speaker impart enthusiasm?

Now please add overleaf any other comments not covered above which will be helpful to the speaker

SELF PRESENTATION
(exercises 50 - 53)

Science education does not generally develop students' skills of self presentation. This means that science students commonly do themselves less than justice when it comes to oral exams, job applications or even telephone conversations.

The exercises in this section give students the opportunity to consider their self presentation and practise the relevant skills.

Applying for jobs 50

Although they may appear to be the least demanding aspect of the business of finding a job, forms and letters of application can cause students considerable problems. We have been worried by the numbers of trivial mistakes which are displayed during this exercise and by the ignorance of fundamental information - such as the name of the head of the department in which a student has been studying for two or three years.

How to run the exercise

a Look through the job advertisements in the appropriate professional journals and select some which suit your students.

b Obtain sufficient copies of the Standard Application Form for each student to have one in class. (These forms are available from your careers section.)

c In the class give your students the details of the jobs available and ask each to choose one. It obviously doesn't matter if several of them go for the same job.

d Hand round the application forms and tell the group that for the purpose of this session they are to use these forms for applying for their chosen job.

e The students then start to fill in the forms and it is helpful if you ask for questions and feedback as each section is completed. It is surprising how quickly hitches arise. They may range from the silly: 'I've just written my surname on the line for first names' to the more problematical: 'When they ask me what salary I expect, should I aim high or offer myself as a bargain they can't refuse?' Even trivial questions can lead to good advice. For example, when enough people have admitted to silly mistakes it becomes obvious that it's a good idea to make a copy of any form so that one can have a practice run. This, of course, also ensures that there is a copy to refer to again before any interview.

f   Even if you have discussed the forms in class point-by-point it is a good idea to take them in and mark them. We have found that the number of careless mistakes and the frequent misunderstanding of some of the questions more than justify giving them individual attention.

Getting the most out of the exercise

a   When you hand their application forms back to the class you could remind everyone that the careers officer will always help a student to prepare an application.

b   You can also extend this exercise by suggesting that the students interview each other on the basis of their completed forms (see exercise 51).

c   You might like to consider asking the careers staff if they would organise a follow-up to this introductory session.

d   Many colleges and polytechnics require their science students to take up a short-term laboratory or industrial post during the course of their training. These placements may last for up to a year and students apply for them independently, going for interview and, to a certain extent, competing with each other for the more popular jobs. One of the advantages of this system is that students go through a genuine process of job application while they still have support and feedback from their teaching staff. If your students will be applying for such placements you could ask the member of staff in charge for a selection of posts which have been offered in the past, and use these for this exercise.

e   You could also find out as much as you can about each placement, the sort of information which is not obvious from the official description. You may be able to interview some of the students who actually worked in these placements in previous years. After your students have completed their application forms you could then make use of any extra information that you have about the jobs they chose. For example, some may involve an extremely repetitive routine (even though the work may be directed towards an interesting goal); some employers may believe that certain jobs are more suited to women (or to men). Find out whether this information would cause any of the group to change the style of their application or even to change their mind about applying for the job at all. This can lead to questions such as 'How might you discover more about an advertised post before you apply, and/or during the interview? How far should you be prepared to try anything? How far should you decide beforehand what you can or cannot do? How can you discover what type of job will really suit you? Such questions can form the basis for subsequent sessions on job applications.

Job interviews 51

Many students go for job interviews without the benefit of any kind of preparation or practice beforehand. This exercise gives your students the opportunity to try out different approaches before the interview and get helpful feedback in a safe situation.

How to run the exercise

a If you have already got students to fill in application forms or write letters of application (see exercise 50) ask them to bring these along to the class to use them as a basis for their interviews.

b Divide the class into groups of three. The members of each group will work in turn as interviewer, interviewee and observer.

c Give instructions to the students in each role:

Interviewees: 'Before the interview starts, tell the interviewer what job you are pretending to be applying for so that he or she knows what kinds of question to ask you. (If any of you have got an interview for a real job coming up, then tell the interviewer about that.)'

Interviewers: 'Ask the interviewees questions about why they want the job and why they think they should get it. Ask them about the course that they're doing and find out what they've gained from it. Try and decide if your interviewee is a suitable candidate for the job'.

Observers: 'Your job is to observe the interviewees and make notes on how they present themselves. Look out for non-verbal as well as verbal communication. [See exercise 5]. Ask yourself whether you would give this person the job and if not why not.

'At the end of the interview, give some feedback to the interviewee. Try to balance positive and negative feedback so that you are offering suggestions for improvement as well as giving credit for good points. And another thing: it's better if your feedback is specific rather than general. For example, it's more helpful to say "I liked the way you looked straight at the interviewer at the start" rather than "You began well".'

d   Allow about 10 minutes for each interview and about 5 minutes for each feedback session (i.e. 45 minutes for this part of the exercise).

e   Encourage students to identify what they have learned. They can do this, for example, in a round: 'One thing I learned about interviews from the feedback I was given'. If they are not used to doing rounds, you will need to explain the ground rules to them:

speak in turn

it's OK to pass

it's OK to repeat what someone else has already said.

You can, if you like, list those contributions on the board under the heading 'How to do well in an interview'.

Telephoning   52

Telephoning skills feature on many communication syllabuses. This is often a response to requests from employers of day-release and sandwich course students: they see efficient telephoning as a crucial skill and appreciate any training which colleges can offer.

The teaching of telephoning skills, however, poses problems. Students rarely believe - or admit - that they have anything to learn about telephoning and so approach exercises such as role play with little enthusiasm.

One way of handling this is to get students to see themselves as trainers rather than trainees. If you ask them to identify the telephoning skills needed by newcomers to a job, they can do this without feeling that their own competence is under attack. If in addition they are required to do the exercise as a test question, this will ensure that they take it seriously.

Another benefit of this exercise is that it offers an opportunity to make a link with any work on non-verbal communication which the students may have done (see exercise 5).

Telephoning

Q. What are the problems in communicating by telephone? Draw up a set of guidelines to help a new colleague to answer the telephone efficiently and professionally at your place of work.

Oral exams 53

Oral exams and tests are used to assess students on many science courses. This can be a frightening experience for the students and one in which they often do not do themselves justice, usually because they are inadequately prepared.

You can be helpful to your students by giving them the opportunity to practise the skills needed for oral exams. One way you can do this is by setting up a role play exercise. (You don't need to be a science teacher for this because students generate their own material.)

How to run the exercise

You could say:

a 'First, can you get into groups of three/four/five?' (The size of group will depend on the number of people - examiners and candidates - who are normally involved in an oral exam on the course.)

b 'Now I'd like you all to write down some questions that might be asked in an oral exam. And some answers too. If you've already sat an oral exam you may be able to remember some of the questions you were asked; if not, you can invent your own. Use your lecture notes if you want to. You need to write down at least as many questions as there are other people in your group. You've got 5 minutes to do this.'

c 'Now each group choose one person to go first in the role of candidate. OK, candidates, you're going to leave the room and wait outside the door while the other members of your group prepare to examine you. Right, see you in a few minutes.'

d   'Right, examiners, what you do now is choose a question each to ask the candidate. Then decide on the order in which you're going to put your questions. You can rearrange the furniture, too, if you like. And do anything else which you think will make it seem more real before the candidates come back in.'

e   'You can come in now, candidates. What you're going to do next is go back to your groups and try to answer the questions they put to you. You've got 5 minutes for this.' (The time allowance for this part of the exercise can be increased as students gain confidence.)

f   'Now can the examiners in each group give feedback to the candidate? Give him or her a grade if you want to. Will 5 minutes be enough for this?'

Getting the most out of the exercise

a   You can give the students information about the typical behaviour of examiners on their course. This can be given to groups at the point when the candidates are out of the room. If you don't know what this information is because you are not normally involved in oral exams you will need to ask permission to attend some exams as an observer.

b   You can help students to give each other useful feedback by prompting them to comment on each other's self presentation, manner, fluency etc. and not just on their answers to their questions (though an incidental benefit of this exercise is that students often get engrossed in discussing the material in a way which is rarely seen in seminars). You can also remind them that a balance of positive and negative points is the most constructive kind of criticism. You may even want to give them a format for their feedback, perhaps in the form of a written report. It could look something like this:

Name of candidate ....

Number of questions answered correctly.........................

Two positive points about your self presentation..........

....

....

Two suggestions for improvement...................................

....

....

c   If students feel anxious about oral exams they will also experience some anxiety in doing this exercise. This anxiety may be expressed indirectly: for example, laughter may be used as tension release. It is important that you allow your students the opportunity to express their anxiety in any way they choose. You can do this by giving them the chance to talk things over and by showing that you realise that the oral exam is a threatening experience.

d   You can help your students to specify what they've learned at the end of the exercise. They may find this difficult if this is their first experience of role play but they need to be aware of what they've learned if they are to benefit fully from the experience. A simple way of highlighting this is to do a round of the whole class in which each student in turn identifies 'One thing I've learned from this exercise' or 'One piece of advice I would give to students taking oral exams'. This will bring everyone together at the end of the session and give students the opportunity to hear all the other contributions.

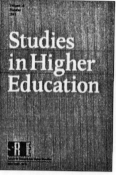